HELEN

THE EVOLUTION FROM DIVINE TO HEROIC IN GREEK EPIC TRADITION

MNEMOSYNE
BIBLIOTHECA CLASSICA BATAVA

COLLEGERUNT

W. DEN BOER • W. J. VERDENIUS • R. E. H. WESTENDORP BOERMA

BIBLIOTHECAE FASCICULOS EDENDOS CURAVIT

W. J. VERDENIUS, HOMERUSLAAN 53, ZEIST

SUPPLEMENTUM QUADRAGESIMUM SECUNDUM

LINDA LEE CLADER

HELEN

THE EVOLUTION FROM DIVINE TO HEROIC
IN GREEK EPIC TRADITION

LUGDUNI BATAVORUM E. J. BRILL MCMLXXVI

HELEN

THE EVOLUTION FROM DIVINE TO HEROIC IN GREEK EPIC TRADITION

BY

LINDA LEE CLADER

LUGDUNI BATAVORUM E. J. BRILL MCMLXXVI

ISBN 90 04 04721 2

Copyright 1976 by E. J. Brill, Leiden, Netherlands

All rights reserved. No part of this book may be reproduced or translated in any form, by print, photoprint, microfilm, microfiche or any other means without written permission from the publisher

PRINTED IN THE NETHERLANDS

FOR MY PARENTS

TABLE OF CONTENTS

Acknowledgements IX
Note on the Spelling of Proper Names X

Introduction 1
   I. Helen in the *Iliad* 5
  II. Helen in the *Odyssey* 24
 III. The Character of Helen in Epic Diction 41
 IV. Helen's Divine Nature Outside of Homeric Poetry 63

Conclusion 81

Indexes 84
  1. General Index 84
  2. Greek Words 88
  3. Principal Passages Cited 89

ACKNOWLEDGEMENTS

I would like to express my gratitude to the many teachers, students, and friends who, during informal conversations or through formal reading and evaluation, have given me insights into some ways to deal with Helen. I owe a special debt of thanks to Emily Vermeule and Cedric Whitman, who criticized the first drafts; to Deborah Dickmann Boedecker, Douglas Frame, Leonard Muellner, and Richard Shannon, who were especially supportive along the way; to Geraldine Clader, who helped edit the final draft; and to Gregory Nagy, who provided inspiration, enthusiasm and keen criticism from the beginning of the project until it took this final form.

A NOTE ON THE SPELLING OF PROPER NAMES

In a futile effort to remain consistent in my translation of Greek names into English I have followed the general practice of retaining the Greek spellings whenever practicable, and adopting a Latinized form only when the name has become so familiar in English that to spell it in pure transliterated Greek would hinder, rather than aid, identification.

INTRODUCTION

> Helen ... is one of the most plausible examples of a "faded" goddess, i.e., one whose original deity has been forgotten, and who has been consequently made into a mortal woman in mythology.
>
> H. J. Rose and C. M. Robertson [1]
>
> The two objections to the whole of this goddess-theory are in the first place that it is sterile; in the second that it is unnatural: sterile because it utterly fails to explain that which alone interests us, the epic career of Helen, for which there are no real analogies in the legends of moon-goddesses and earth-goddesses in any known mythologies: unnatural because ... it reverses the order of the evidence, the earliest testimony pointing to the humanity of Helen, while we cannot find evidence for her divinity earlier than the prophecy of Euripides at the close of the *Orestes*.
>
> L. R. Farnell [2]

When the study of the history of religion began to take shape as an established discipline, the tendency was to ignore Greek mythology as legitimate evidence because of its artistic context; Martin Nilsson, a master in the field, was inclined to be suspicious of literary evidence and preferred, where possible, to confine himself to information on pure cult and ritual. More recently, however, Georges Dumézil and Stig Wikander have begun to explore the relationship between literary myth and religious history, specifically as exemplified in Indo-Iranian epic. This body of epic material is of Indo-European origin, and thus can be seen as comparable to Homeric epic not only typologically, but genetically. Dumézil and Wikander have provided an approach which makes it possible to handle an epic figure in terms of his own natural surroundings, the epic genre itself.

In his study of the Pāṇḍavas, heroic brothers in the epic Mahābhārata who do not appear in the much earlier Vedas, Wikander has shown that some epic figures represent "anthropomorphisations" of characters who had held a central position in a mythological

---

[1] *Oxford Classical Dictionary*, 2nd ed. (Oxford, 1970), s.v. Helen.
[2] *Greek Hero Cults and Ideas of Immortality* (Oxford, 1921), p. 324.

system older than that of Vedic religion.³ In oversimplified terms, he is agreeing with the "faded god" theory of epic, but his study produces a much richer definition of the term than the one offered by Rose and Robertson, above. The divinity of an epic figure is not necessarily "forgotten," but is translated into new terms peculiar to the epic *genre*.

The student of Greek epic is in a less secure position than Wikander for dealing with "faded gods," for extant oral Greek epic represents a late stage of mythological and artistic development, a stage where the mythology is highly synthesized and has been largely transformed from an active expression of living religious belief into an artistic *genre*. In the case of Helen, then, the earliest evidence of her existence might seem to be of no help in determining her original nature. As Farnell has suggested, Homer's portrayal of the lady does appear to point toward her humanity, or at least to the possibility that she is entirely the result of a flash of poetic inspiration. Helen has her own personality and role to play in epic, and would seem to function simply as a character within a story. Nevertheless, scrutiny of the figure of Helen in the epics themselves is rewarded with traces—and at the late stage of development Homer represents, traces are of great value—of her prior existence as a divine entity. Some of this evidence emerges directly from a close look at the very activities and dialogues in which the Homeric lady engages; some is more subtle and must be approached through the method inaugurated by Milman Parry and Albert Lord, and elaborated upon by Michael Nagler and William Whallon,⁴ the study of oral epic diction. Once the original Helen has been glimpsed by dealing directly with the Homeric corpus, her nature can be outlined more clearly with the aid of later cult evidence and linguistic considerations.

The original Helen discovered, a Homeric problem still presents itself: how did Helen the divine figure become involved in a war-saga, and why does the oral epic tradition choose to treat her as a

---

³ S. Wikander, "La Légende des Pāṇḍava et la substructure mythique du Mahābhārata," trans. G. Dumézil, *Jupiter, Mars, Quirinus* IV (Bibliothèque de l'école des hautes études, Sciences religieuses 52, Paris, 1948), pp. 47-48.

⁴ M. Parry, "L'Épithète traditionelle dans Homère (Paris, 1928), trans. in M. Parry, *The Making of Homeric Verse* (Oxford, 1971); A. B. Lord, especially *The Singer of Tales* (Harvard, 1960); M. Nagler, "Towards a Generative View of the Oral Formula," *TAPA* 98 (1967) 269-311; W. Whallon, "The Homeric Epithets," *YCS* 17 (1961) 97-142, and *Formula, Character, and Context: Studies in Homeric, Old English, and Old Testament Poetry* (Harvard, 1969).

"human" heroine instead of a goddess? The work of Dumézil and Wikander may help to answer these questions, but ultimately Homer must be able to answer them himself. What should emerge is a more complete definition—or a step toward the definition—of the heroic nature in epic poetry, Helen serving as an easily accessible example of the manner in which that nature may have developed.

CHAPTER ONE

HELEN IN THE *ILIAD*

In developing a unified work of art out of a vast tradition, the poet of the *Iliad* is faced with the necessity of subordinating a great deal of his material to the major themes of his work. Individual characters may have a wealth of information or history traditionally surrounding them, but in the context of the *Iliad* they fulfill specialized functions for the sake of artistic unity. For example, while Ajax has his own heroic tradition, including many episodes with which Homer does not deal in the surviving epic, his role in the *Iliad* is several times specifically drawn to contrast with Achilles: at I 622 ff, he is the last, simplest, and still most convincing of the members of the Embassy, arguing from the standpoint of loyalty to one's friends; at Π 101 ff, immediately after Achilles' outburst of prayer that only he and Patroklos be spared death at Troy, the scene dramatically shifts to Ajax, the exhausted bulwark who will not give way as the Trojans prepare to burn the Achaian ships. Thus while Achilles withdraws further and further from human society and any feeling of duty to his comrades, Ajax stands as the constant reminder of exactly what the traditional heroic ethic requires.

Such is the case with Helen. Given a vast bulk of material about a Spartan lady who appeared as the central figure in numerous heroic adventures,[1] Homer selects a few aspects of her nature and history to round out as significant to the themes upon which he is concentrating. The major theme in the *Iliad*, to which all else is subordinated, is the Wrath of Achilles.[2] In dealing with Helen's role in this epic, then, one must determine not so much what she has to do with the Trojan War, but specifically what she has to do with Achilles.

One of the expressions of Achilles' heroic dilemma comes at I 412-416, where he mentions the two possible destinies awaiting him:

---

[1] See Chapter Four, pp. 71-75 for a list of her known adventures.
[2] For a discussion of the centrality of the Wrath to the *Iliad*, see C. H. Whitman, *Homer and the Heroic Tradition* (Harvard, 1958), pp. 181-220.

εἰ μέν κ' αὖθι μένων Τρώων πόλιν ἀμφιμάχωμαι,
ὤλετο μέν μοι νόστος, ἀτὰρ κλέος ἄφθιτον ἔσται·
εἰ δέ κεν οἴκαδ' ἵκωμι φίλην ἐς πατρίδα γαῖαν,
ὤλετό μοι κλέος ἐσθλόν, ἐπὶ δηρὸν δέ μοι αἰὼν
ἔσσεται, οὐδέ κέ μ' ὦκα τέλος θανάτοιο κιχείη.

Only if he remains to fight will he receive κλέος, a place among the ranks of the heroes in epic poetry.[3] Homer identifies Achilles with poetry, then, through his dilemma. Implicitly, the fact that the audience has heard of Achilles shows that in the end he did choose κλέος over νόστος. Homer further strengthens the identification with poetry by having Achilles sing the κλέα ἀνδρῶν to himself. This is a self-conscious poetic touch, for the subject of Achilles' song should be the deeds happening around him, and he should be a part of those deeds. Achilles is drawn as aware of the poetic implications of κλέος, and thus his decision between κλέος and νόστος is in part a self-conscious reference to epic and even the epic presently being performed.

What, then, does Helen have to do with Achilles? On the surface, she is the reason for his being in Troy along with all the other Achaians (e.g. B 161, 177, I 339, T 325). They have come to rescue her for Menelaos. Less obviously, however, the warriors at Troy are also there to win κλέος, as Homer says directly more than once (e.g. Λ 227, N 364). They are, like Achilles, concerned with becoming material for epic poetry.

It is significant that all of Helen's appearances in the *Iliad* are associated with poetry. Homer prepares for her first entrance by crystallizing the reason for the War in the duel of Paris and Menelaos. Here for the first time in the *Iliad* the basis of the conflict is being acted out: the wronged husband, backed by his supporters, confronts the treacherous guest, backed by his. To make the point of their contest even more apparent, Homer places their prize above them on the Wall of Troy.

Iris arrives at Helen's megaron to summon her to the Wall and finds her weaving:

... ἡ δὲ μέγαν ἱστὸν ὕφαινε,
δίπλακα πορφυρέην, πολέας δ' ἐνέπασσεν ἀέθλους

---

[3] On κλέος as a symbol for epic poetry, see G. Nagy, *Comparative Studies in Greek and Indic Metre* (Harvard, 1974), especially pp. 229-261.

Τρώων θ' ἱπποδάμων καὶ 'Αχαιῶν χαλκοχιτώνων,
οὕς ἕθεν εἵνεκ' ἔπασχον ὑπ' "Αρηος παλαμάων (Γ 125-128).

An ἄεθλος is often a contest specifically for a prize (e.g. Ψ 707, etc., and φ 180, where Penelope is the prize), and in the *Iliad* the word occurs only here meaning "struggle." [4] Indeed, Helen is the prize of the present battle, and so the weaving she is doing has direct reference to the very scene about to be enacted outside the walls, the duel between Paris and Menelaos for possession of her. She is weaving the figures on a background πορφυρέην, the color of death,[5] for the subject of her artistry is not only heroic, but also deadly. Dramatically, of course, Helen cannot yet know what is happening outside, and thematically the only epic character who can have knowledge unmotivated by the action is the ἀοιδός, the bard.[6] Helen acts overtly as a bard at δ 238 ff,[7] but here at Γ 125-128 the connection is much less obvious. Nevertheless, the very activity which occupies her provides the key to the problem.

Marcello Durante has shown that in Indo-European tradition weaving is a symbol of poetic composition.[8] Homer himself lends

---

[4] Π 590 f, in fact, specifically distinguishes πόλεμος from ἄεθλος. For further analysis of the duel, see J. Th. Kakridis, *Homer Revisited* (Publications of the New Society of Letters at Lund 64, 1971), pp. 34 ff.

[5] Whitman, p. 118 and n. 39.

[6] Cf. B 484-493; Detienne makes the following comment on this subject: "Par sa mémoire, le poète accède directement, dans une vision personelle, aux événements qu'il évoque; il a le privilège d'entrer en contact avec l'autre monde. Sa mémoire lui permet de 'déchiffrer l'invisible.' " (M. Detienne, *Les maîtres de vérité dans la Grèce archaïque*, Paris: Maspero, 1967, p. 15); cf. also J. P. Vernant, "Aspects mythiques de la mémoire en Grèce," *Journal de Psychologie* 56 (1959) 1-29; this article is also incorporated in his *Mythe et Pensée chez les Grecs: Études de psychologie historique*, 2nd ed. (Paris: Maspero, 1969) pp. 51-78; also J. A. Scott, *The Unity of Homer* (Berkeley: U. Cal. Press, 1921), pp. 128-134.

[7] See pp. 32 ff.

[8] "Ricerche sulla preistoria della lingua poetica greca. La terminologia relativa alla creazione poetica," *Atti della Accademia Nazionale dei Lincei*, Serie ottava, Rendiconti, Classe di Scienze morali, storiche e filologiche 15 (1960) 238-244. (Pp. 231-249 of this article are translated into German in R. Schmitt, *Indogermanische Dichtersprache*, Darmstadt, Wissenschaftliche Buchgesellschaft, 1968, pp. 261-290.) Cf. also R. Schmitt, *Dichtung und Dichtersprache in indo-germanische Zeit* (Wiesbaden: Harrassowitz, 1967), p. 300; also the Hesiodic fragment

ἐν Δήλῳ τότε πρῶτον ἐγὼ καὶ "Ομηρος ἀοιδοί

support to this theory, for he portrays both Kirke and Kalypso as singing while they weave:

... ἡ δ' ἔνδον ἀοιδιάουσ' ὀπὶ καλῇ
ἱστὸν ἐποιχομένη χρυσείῃ κερκίδ' ὕφαινεν (ε 61-62),

Κίρκης δ' ἔνδον ἄκουον ἀειδούσης ὀπὶ καλῇ,
ἱστὸν ἐποιχομένης μέγαν ἄμβροτον ... (κ 221-222),

... ἔνδον γάρ τις ἐποιχομένη μέγαν ἱστὸν
καλὸν ἀοιδιάει ... (κ 226-227).

Two of these passages (ε 61, κ 227) contain the only uses of the verb ἀοιδιάω in Homer, which is thus strangely restricted to the weaving theme. Kirke and Kalypso weave no pictures into their webs, but they do sing; Helen does not sing, but does weave a tapestry with figures, an action which recalls Simonides' statement where he defines

τὴν μὲν ζωγραφίαν ποίησιν σιωπῶσαν ... τὴν δὲ ποίησιν ζωγραφίαν λαλοῦσαν.[9]

The vision of Helen at her loom, then, seems to be a profoundly self-conscious statement by the singer. Within the context of the action, Helen is both author and subject of her work. Moreover, the scene draws attention to her position in the entire tradition. She is working in designs of struggling warriors, weaving the very fabric of heroic epic. Later, when Hektor has come to the house of Paris to urge him back to battle, Helen calls herself, Paris and Hektor ἀοίδιμοι ἐσσομένοισι (Ζ 358), subjects of oral poetry. This is the only use of ἀοίδιμος in epic, and the implication would be that as figures of song Helen and those connected with her are especially singled out. Thus Homer is using Helen's poetic self-consciousness on two levels: within the drama she is aware of her role as Cause of War, and she also embodies the poet's awareness of the nature of his craft. The most beautiful woman in the epic world creates a piece of art which is itself a symbol of poetry. Homer must see himself not as the creator of Helen, but as an artist in a position both above and

---

μέλπομεν, ἐν νεαροῖς ὕμνοις ῥάψαντες ἀοιδήν,
Φοῖβον Ἀπόλλωνα χρυσάορον, ὃν τέκε Λητώ (fr. 357 M/W);

also W. B. Stanford, *Greek Metaphor* (Oxford, 1936, reprinted by Johnson Reprint, New York, 1972), p. 130, on the relationship of ὑφαίνω to ὕμνος.

[9] Plutarch, *De Gloria Atheniensium* 3; cf. Detienne, pp. 105-109.

below her in tradition. She is woven into his picture, but she also has a preexistence before the *Iliad* which implies that in some measure she has woven the picture around herself.[10]

Helen's role in the *Teichoskopia* fills out this aspect of her Homeric character even further. She is the author of what is essentially a second catalogue, almost immediately following the first. This one is of a different nature from the Catalogue of Ships, however, which is careful to attach each hero to a city and each city to a hero. Helen's catalogue does not care so much for geography. The descriptions of the heroes concentrate on their specifically heroic qualities, not on the host they rule. Curiously, in this scene the quality comes first, as Priam perceives it; Helen attaches it to a hero, and the theme is then elaborated. Thus Priam asks who that man is who looks so lordly; Helen answers that it is

... εὐρὺ κρείων 'Αγαμέμνων,
ἀμφότερον βασιλεύς τ' ἀγαθὸς κρατερός τ' αἰχμητής (Γ 178-179),

and then Priam elaborates on Agamemnon's lordliness with an example. The hero is not identified as king of Mycenae, but simply as kingly. Similarly, Ajax is πελώριος, ἕρκος 'Αχαιῶν (229) but not Salaminian.[11] Although Odysseus and Idomeneus are located at Ithaca and Crete, their central identifications here are as trickster and guest-friend of Menelaos, respectively. Besides Agamemnon's lordliness, the one other characteristic which Helen mentions is that he was once her brother-in-law. In some measure, then, she is identifying the heroes by their relationship to her.

It is striking that a woman should be the poet of a catalogue of this sort. Traditionally, such a scene should be dominated by a member of the opposing side, who could provide information about his former comrades on the basis of his own martial experience.[12]

---

[10] Note that Andromache learns of Hektor's death while weaving in the book balancing Γ, X 437 ff, and that the diction, too, is exactly parallel. Cf. C. Segal, "Andromache's Anagnoresis." *HSCP* 75 (1971) 40.

[11] M. Parry, *The Making of Homeric Verse* (Oxford, 1971), pp. 157 f, shows that πελώριος is never ornamental; thus Homer's use of the epithet here stresses the quality.

[12] Cf. C. O'Rahilly, ed., *Táin Bó Cúalnge* (Dublin: Dublin Institute for Advanced Studies, 1967), pp. 156-158. King Aillil and Queen Medb question the exile Fergus about the opposing host; cf. also "The Intoxication of the Ulstermen" in T. P. Cross and C. H. Slover, *Ancient Irish Tales* (New York: Holt, 1936), pp. 226 ff. The exile Cú Roi tells Aillil and Mebd about Conchobar and his host; Cú Roi had previously fought on the side of Conchobar.

Most of Helen's descriptions could have been given just as well by an Achaian warrior as by her,[13] and the question remains why Homer chose to have her, a woman, introduce the great leaders. A quick consideration of how she knows them in the first place may provide a clue. Helen could not have traveled through Greece meeting the heroes, but at one time they did travel to Sparta to see her, the time when they all competed as suitors for her hand.[14] Now, in the Hesiodic account of the heroes arriving at Sparta there are two conspicuous absences—Menelaos, who sent his brother to woo Helen for him,

... ἀλλ' Ἀγαμέμνων
γαμβρὸς ἐὼν ἐμνᾶτο κασιγνήτῳ Μενελάῳ (fr. 197. 4-5, M/W),

and Achilles, who was still too young to be a suitor:

... Χείρων δ' ἐν Πηλίῳ ὑλήεντι
Πηλείδην ἐκόμιζε πόδας ταχύν, ἔξοχον ἀνδρῶν,
παῖδ' ἔτ' ἐόντ'· (fr. 204. 87-89, M/W).

It is curious that these two heroes are also left out of the *Teichoskopia*. Menelaos should be no more familiar to Priam than Odysseus (Γ 204 ff), nor should the absence of Achilles, greatest of the Greek warriors, be less conspicuous than that of Kastor and Polydeukes (Γ 236 ff). The audience knows, of course, that Achilles is not present at the duel because he is sulking in his tent, but Helen and Priam have not been apprised of this fact. A possible explanation may be that Menelaos and Achilles were not suitors, and so traditionally Helen could not catch sight of them coming to fight for her.

The *Teichoskopia*, then, is a reminder that the Trojan War is a second contest for possession of Argive Helen. The conspicuous absence of Achilles from both lists of heroes now carries some implication regarding his withdrawal from battle. Because he was never one of Helen's suitors, his reason for coming to Troy must have been primarily to gain κλέος and only secondarily to rescue Helen.[15] For Achilles, Helen must be simply a symbol of the epic

---

Cf. also the story of Dolon, who gives a little catalogue of the Trojans (K 426-431).

[13] It seems to be traditional for the informant to be an exile (e.g., Fergus) or renegade (Sinon in *Aeneid* II. 57 ff is of this tradition) from the opposition.

[14] For the list of suitors, see Hesiod fr. 196 ff M/W.

[15] The Hesiodic "Oath of the Suitors" (M/W fr. 204. 78 ff) may be a reflection of the Trojan War situation, explaining why all the Achaians

quest, a symbol of the κλέος which must be a hero's ultimate goal. His equation of the love of the Atreidai for Helen with his love for Briseis (I 334-343) shows that he is aware of the distinction he is making in his anger, that he places the campaign for Helen in perspective. He is never haunted by the question of whether his failure to fight will lose Helen to the Trojans; his delemma is whether or not to continue pursuing κλέος.

Helen's last appearance in the *Iliad*, where she sings the final lament at Hektor's funeral (Ω 761-776), is another hint at her symbolic position in the poet's mind. Why should Helen, who is only Hektor's sister-in-law, hold the most prominent place in the sequence? If Homer had been looking for just anyone to round out a trio of mourners, he might have chosen Kassandra or another of Hektor's sisters. Helen is clearly included for a special purpose, for her position as the last mourner also places her within thirty lines of the end of the epic, and in fact she does have the last long speech in the *Iliad*. One reason for her prominent position must be that just as Homer begins the epic with the Cause of the Wrath (A 8), it is appropriate that he end it with a statement by the Cause of the War. Moreover, the death of Hektor represents the death of Troy, and also implies the death of Achilles.[16] If Helen is, indeed, associated with the heroic quest for κλέος, then it is only right that she should sing a dirge for the hero who has died for her. The progression among the three laments is quite formal, each one ending with a statement of its effect on the people.[17] Andromache's moves the women (Ω 746), Hekabe's γόον δ' ἀλίαστον ὄρινε (760), but Helen's moves the whole δῆμος to mourning (776). In effect the laments of the three women at Hektor's funeral represent the beginnings of the memorial of oral poetry that the heroes have won. Coming at the very end of an epic, they are also a reference to the composition which has just been performed.

It appears, then, that in the *Iliad* Helen represents the heroic quest, overtly a quest for possession of Helen the woman, latently for possession of κλέος. Wherever she appears she is accompanied by poetry or even creates it herself. The irresistibility of such a charac-

---

came with Menelaos. This possibility has no bearing on the question of which tradition came first—Helen's suitors or the *Teichoskopia*. By the time of Homer both traditions were certainly established.
[16] See Whitman, p. 156.
[17] C. Segal, p. 37.

ter lies not only in her beauty but also in the immortality which she can symbolically bestow. Yet this immortality comes at a price—paradoxically, often death—and the price is what Achilles struggles with in his choice between νόστος and κλέος:

οὐ γὰρ ἐμοὶ ψυχῆς ἀντάξιον οὐδ' ὅσα φασὶν
Ἴλιον ἐκτῆσθαι . . .
ἀνδρὸς δὲ ψυχὴ πάλιν ἐλθεῖν οὔτε λεϊστὴ
οὔθ' ἑλετή, ἐπεὶ ἄρ κεν ἀμείψεται ἕρκος ὀδόντων (Ι 401-409).[18]

For Achilles, as it has been remarked, the choice must be between νόστος and κλέος, with Helen only a visible symbol of one alternative. Homer makes Achilles' choice even more starkly defined by drawing Helen as a dangerous woman, with the same sinister beauty which κλέος, won through suffering and death, portends for the hero. For all her attractiveness, she remains the lady who fled from her husband with a foreign lover, and who thus brought tragic war upon Troy and Argos.

This theme is expressed most dramatically by the elders on the Wall as they see Helen approaching:

οὐ νέμεσις Τρῶας καὶ ἐϋκνήμιδας Ἀχαιοὺς
τοιῇδ' ἀμφὶ γυναικὶ πολὺν χρόνον ἄλγεα πάσχειν·
αἰνῶς ἀθανάτῃσι θεῇς εἰς ὦπα ἔοικεν·
ἀλλὰ καὶ ὣς τοίη περ ἐοῦσ' ἐν νηυσὶ νεέσθω,
μηδ' ἡμῖν τεκέεσσί τ' ὀπίσσω πῆμα λίποιτο (Γ 156-160).

This statement is the closest Homer ever comes to a physical description of the most beautiful woman in the world: αἰνῶς ἀθανάτῃσι θεῇς εἰς ὦπα ἔοικεν. Traditionally, it is dangerous for a man to come face to face with a goddess, for he is liable to leave the encounter crippled or unmanned.[19] The simile employed by the elders is thus an expression more of Helen's effect on them than of any objective quality in her.[20] She is at once irresistibly attractive and terrible to behold.

Helen's dangerous nature is in part personified in Aphrodite. When the goddess in disguise approaches Helen to summon her to Paris' bedchamber following the duel, Helen becomes angry at the thought, recognizes Aphrodite and reacts stubbornly:

[18] Cf. I 316-322.
[19] Cf. e.g., Anchises' speech to Aphrodite, H. Ven. 181-190.
[20] For a discussion of αἰνῶς as a term applied to goddesses, see A. Amory, "The Gates of Horn and Ivory," YCS 20 (1966) 29 ff.

δαιμονίη, τί με ταῦτα λιλαίεαι ἠπεροπεύειν;
ἦ πή με προτέρω πολίων εὖ ναιομενάων
ἄξεις, ἢ Φρυγίης ἢ Μηονίης ἐρατεινῆς,
εἴ τίς τοι καὶ κεῖθι φίλος μερόπων ἀνθρώπων·
οὕνεκα δὴ νῦν δῖον 'Αλέξανδρον Μενέλαος
νικήσας ἐθέλει στυγερὴν ἐμὲ οἴκαδ' ἄγεσθαι,
τοὔνεκα δὴ νῦν δεῦρο δολοφρονέουσα παρέστης;
ἧσο παρ' αὐτὸν ἰοῦσα, θεῶν δ' ἀπόεικε κελεύθου,
μηδ' ἔτι σοῖσι πόδεσσιν ὑποστρέψειας Ὄλυμπον,
ἀλλ' αἰεὶ περὶ κεῖνον ὀΐζυε καί ἑ φύλασσε,
εἰς ὅ κέ σ' ἢ ἄλοχον ποιήσεται, ἢ ὅ γε δούλην.
κεῖσε δ' ἐγὼν οὐκ εἶμι — νεμεσσητὸν δέ κεν εἴη —
κείνου πορσανέουσα λέχος· Τρῳαὶ δέ μ' ὀπίσσω
πᾶσαι μωμήσονται· ἔχω δ' ἄχε' ἄκριτα θυμῷ (Γ 399-412).

If Helen's reference to other cities be taken as a Homeric glance at the larger abduction legend surrounding her, then she is showing justifiable exasperation with Aphrodite, who is the motivation behind such activities. Nevertheless, no other Homeric character rebukes a divinity in such strong language, and the implication must be that Helen and the goddess are uncommonly close. Following Helen's objection, Aphrodite reacts angrily with a threat to desert her:

μή μ' ἔρεθε, σχετλίη, μὴ χωσαμένη σε μεθείω,
τὼς δέ σ' ἀπεχθήρω ὡς νῦν ἔκπαγλα φίλησα,
μέσσῳ δ' ἀμφοτέρων μητίσομαι ἔχθεα λυγρά,
Τρώων καὶ Δαναῶν, σὺ δέ κεν κακὸν οἶτον ὄληαι (Γ 414-417).

Aphrodite is in effect cruelly reminding Helen of her ambiguous position in the War, and pointing out to her that without a goddess' aid she is doomed. Helen is frightened into submission and goes to join Paris.

The scene between Helen and Paris in his bedchamber is a manifestation of Aphrodite's power. Having pulled up a chair for Helen to sit in (Γ 424-425), the goddess disappears from view, but her influence remains. Helen's longing for Menelaos has just been reawakened (Γ 139-140), and she makes an attempt to despise Paris, taunting him with cowardice and wishing he had died under Menelaos' spear (Γ 428-436). But she fails in the end:

> ... ἀλλά σ' ἔγωγε
> παύεσθαι κέλομαι, μηδὲ ξανθῷ Μενελάῳ
> ἀντίβιον πόλεμον πολεμίζειν ἠδὲ μάχεσθαι
> ἀφραδέως, μή πως τάχ' ὑπ' αὐτοῦ δουρὶ δαμήῃς (Γ 433-436).

Paris answers her reproof with an overt proposition:

> μή με, γύναι, χαλεποῖσιν ὀνείδεσι θυμὸν ἔνιπτε·
> νῦν μὲν γὰρ Μενέλαος ἐνίκησεν σὺν Ἀθήνῃ,
> κεῖνον δ' αὖτις ἐγώ· πάρα γὰρ θεοί εἰσι καὶ ἡμῖν.
> ἀλλ' ἄγε δὴ φιλότητι τραπείομεν εὐνηθέντε·
> οὐ γάρ πώ ποτέ μ' ὧδέ γ' ἔρως φρένας ἀμφεκάλυψεν,
> οὐδ' ὅτε σε πρῶτον Λακεδαίμονος ἐξ ἐρατεινῆς
> ἔπλεον ἁρπάξας ἐν ποντοπόροισι νέεσσι,
> νήσῳ δ' ἐν Κραναῇ ἐμίγην φιλότητι καὶ εὐνῇ,
> ὥς σεο νῦν ἔραμαι καί με γλυκὺς ἵμερος αἱρεῖ (Γ 438-446).

This is powerful desire, personally contrived by Aphrodite and controlling the most beautiful of the Trojan women and her beautiful consort. Only one other time in Homer is such strong desire described, in the story of Hera's deception of Zeus. There, too, Aphrodite plays an active role, lending Hera her ἱμάς as a love charm (Ξ 216-221). As Zeus succumbs, he makes a speech similar to that of Paris:

> νῶϊ δ' ἄγ' ἐν φιλότητι τραπείομεν εὐνηθέντε.
> οὐ γάρ πώ ποτέ μ' ὧδε θεᾶς ἔρος οὐδὲ γυναικὸς
> θυμὸν ἐνὶ στήθεσσι περιπροχυθεὶς ἐδάμασσεν,
> οὐδ' ὁπότ' ἠρασάμην Ἰξιονίης ἀλόχοιο,
> ἣ τέκε Πειρίθοον, θεόφιν μήστωρ' ἀτάλαντον·
> οὐδ' ὅτε περ Δανάης καλλισφύρου Ἀκρισιώνης,
> ἣ τέκε Περσῆα, πάντων ἀριδείκετον ἀνδρῶν·
> οὐδ' ὅτε Φοίνικος κούρης τηλεκλειτοῖο,
> ἣ τέκε μοι Μίνων τε καὶ ἀντίθεον Ῥαδάμανθυν·
> οὐδ' ὅτε περ Σεμέλης οὐδ' Ἀλκμήνης ἐνὶ Θήβῃ,
> ἥ ῥ' Ἡρακλῆα κρατερόφρονα γείνατο παῖδα·
> ἣ δὲ Διώνυσον Σεμέλη τέκε, χάρμα βροτοῖσιν·
> οὐδ' ὅτε Δήμητρος καλλιπλοκάμοιο ἀνάσσης,
> οὐδ' ὁπότε Λητοῦς ἐρικυδέος, οὐδὲ σεῦ αὐτῆς,
> ὡς σέο νῦν ἔραμαι καί με γλυκὺς ἵμερος αἱρεῖ (Ξ 314-328).

Nowhere else in Homer is a love-scene so described. There are other lovers in the epics, to be sure—Odysseus and Penelope, Achilles and Briseis, Hektor and Andromache, to name the most obvious—but these two passages in the *Iliad* are the only two where Aphrodite takes so active a part. Moreover, the only parallel to the Helen-Paris scene is a situation of deception, with Aphrodite an accomplice to Hera's plot. The relationships in the scene at hand are analogous, though reversed: Paris is trying to seduce Helen, and Aphrodite's aid makes it impossible for her to refuse. Homer has placed Helen in a hopelessly compromised situation. Although she regrets having left her husband Menelaos and her home and family, she is powerless to resist the beauty of Paris. Aphrodite, goddess of desire, is too strong.

In a sense both appearances of Helen up to this point are building to the climax of Z 312 ff, where the relationship between the two lovers is thrown into contrast with that of Hektor and Andromache. Hektor, the very personification of courage and loyalty to his fatherland—indeed, as Whitman has noted,[21] a symbol of Troy itself— approaches the man and woman who have brought the war upon him and his people. They themselves seem not in the least concerned with the affairs surrounding them, but the warrior-husband sits among Helen and her maidservants in the bedchamber, fondling his beautiful armor. The surface contrast between Hektor and Paris is immediate. Hektor is described in terms of glorious warstrength:

ἔνθ' Ἕκτωρ εἰσῆλθε Διΐ φίλος, ἐν δ' ἄρα χειρὶ
ἔγχος ἔχ' ἑνδεκάπηχυ· πάροιθε δὲ λάμπετο δουρὸς
αἰχμὴ χαλκείη, περὶ δὲ χρύσεος θέε πόρκης (Z 318-320).

He wears the symbols of his courage, while Paris merely plays with his breastplate, spear and bow (Z 321-322). Hektor reproaches him for hanging back from battle, mentioning how many of the Trojans are perishing around the city because of him. The situation is almost a parody of Achilles nursing his anger while he remains in his tent, and indeed, Hektor begins the reproach with words that apply to Achilles far better than to Paris:

δαιμόνι', οὐ μὲν καλὰ χόλον τόνδ' ἔνθεο θυμῷ (Z 326).

Achilles has been doing just the same thing in more than one passage (e.g. I 436, 260; Δ 513), but the tone of his anger and refusal to

---

[21] Whitman, p. 156.

fight is quite serious, while the tone of this scene is close to comic—
tragicomic, perhaps, if one considers the enormity of the battle outside contrasted with the folly within the house. Alexander himself extends the parody by declaring that he was not moved by anger, but rather wanted to give himself over to grief (Z 336). The picture that Paris helps paint of himself is that of a spoiled child, incapable of understanding where duty lies or what honest emotion may be.

To point up the contrast between Paris and Hektor, Helen speaks to her brother-in-law with honey-sweet words:

> δᾶερ ἐμεῖο κυνὸς κακομηχάνου ὀκρυοέσσης,
> ὥς μ' ὄφελ' ἤματι τῷ ὅτε με πρῶτον τέκε μήτηρ
> οἴχεσθαι προφέρουσα κακὴ ἀνέμοιο θύελλα
> εἰς ὄρος ἢ εἰς κῦμα πολυφλοίσβοιο θαλάσσης,
> ἔνθα με κῦμ' ἀπόερσε πάρος τάδε ἔργα γενέσθαι.
> αὐτὰρ ἐπεὶ τάδε γ' ὧδε θεοὶ κακὰ τεκμήραντο,
> ἀνδρὸς ἔπειτ' ὤφελλον ἀμείνονος εἶναι ἄκοιτις,
> ὃς ᾔδη νέμεσίν τε καὶ αἴσχεα πόλλ' ἀνθρώπων.
> τούτῳ δ' οὔτ' ἄρ νῦν φρένες ἔμπεδοι οὔτ' ἄρ' ὀπίσσω
> ἔσσονται· τῶ καί μιν ἐπαυρήσεσθαι ὀΐω.
> ἀλλ' ἄγε νῦν εἴσελθε καὶ ἕζεο τῷδ' ἐπὶ δίφρῳ,
> δᾶερ, ἐπεί σε μάλιστα πόνος φρένας ἀμφιβέβηκεν
> εἵνεκ' ἐμεῖο κυνὸς καὶ Ἀλεξάνδρου ἕνεκ' ἄτης,
> οἷσιν ἐπὶ Ζεὺς θῆκε κακὸν μόρον, ὡς καὶ ὀπίσσω
> ἀνθρώποισι πελώμεθ' ἀοίδιμοι ἐσσομένοισι (Z 344-358).

Beginning with her longest, most hyperbolic, and most beautiful escape-metaphor, Helen voices her recognition of the emptiness of her relationship with Paris, wishing she were the wife of an ἀνὴρ ἀμείνων. Homer certainly intends his audience to think of Hektor as an example of what she wishes for, and the contrast between the two brothers grows stronger, until the scene between Hektor and Andromache presents the picture of a full, profound marriage in dramatic opposition to the patently shallow relationship of Helen and Paris.

Helen's patronness Aphrodite has suggested one menacing aspect of Helen's character, her terrible beauty and irresistibility. The scene with Hektor has pointed to another side of her position in the epic: this shallow marriage between Helen and Paris is the cause for which the Trojans are fighting. With Helen's comment that they all suffer so that they may become things of song for future men, Homer sharpens the focus on the tragedy of the conflict and thus the tragic nature of his own poem. He never says that the War is being fought for a phantom, but his use of Helen in the drama suggests an image rather than a rounded personality. Homer wants to make sure that Achilles' life-and-death decision must be over κλέος alone and that the issue is not confused by the presence of a lady to fight for who is as worthy as the abstract κλέος. So in the epic action his Helen is beautiful but empty, the plaything of the truly terrible goddess Aphrodite, the fickle lady who is now tired of the man she followed in flight from her husband.

The diction surrounding Helen in the *Iliad*, however, suggests a character who is more purely menacing, less sympathetic. Helen begins her speech to Hektor at Z 344 with the following words:

δᾶερ ἐμεῖο κυνὸς κακομηχάνου ὀκρυοέσσης . . .

The expression is clearly intended to imply self-reproach, but the threeword list of reproaches is somewhat curious. Helen characterizes herself as a "bitch" four times in Homer (Γ 180, Z 344, Z 356, δ 145), always in contexts where she refers to the shame of her having brought about the War. In his useful essay on dogs in Homer,[22] Manfred Faust has catalogued every occurrence of both literal and metaphorical uses of κύων in the *Iliad* and *Odyssey*. The manner and contexts in which the word is applied to many characters shows beyond doubt that it was meant to be an insult, but the question remains what kind of insult the term conveyed.

Aside from similes and metaphors, κύων occurs in the *Iliad* forty times. Of these, only four refer to a pet animal,[23] one refers to Kerberos,[24] and thirty-five refer to scavenger-dogs feasting on human flesh. Since a major theme of the *Iliad* is death and warfare, it is not surprising that the image of dogs devouring corpses is so common. Yet even in the *Odyssey*, where the action is less violent and the setting more frequently domestic, this same image occurs eight times.[25] For an epic hero, the thought of being prey to dogs before receiving a proper funeral seems to be a major threat; his heroic ethos may in fact require that he die in order to attain a place in epic, but it would be non-heroic to be eaten rather than honored

---

[22] "Die kunstlerische Verwendung von κύων 'Hund' in den homerischen Epen," *Glotta* 48 (1970) 8-31.
[23] A 50, I 545, Σ 581 ff, Ψ 173.
[24] Θ 368.
[25] γ 259, 271; ξ 133; σ 87; φ 363; χ 30, 476; ω 292.

with an appropriate funeral pyre. In other words, dogs often seem to represent an obstacle in the traditional hero's path to an honorable death.[26]

The fact that Helen calls herself a κύων always in the context of the Trojan War would suggest that the basis of her self-reproach may be connected with the terrible threat that dogs represent to heroes. Perhaps consideration of the rest of the line in her speech to Hektor will help to round out the implication. κακομήχανος occurs only three times in Homer, including the Helen-passage. Once it is in Odysseus' version of the farewell speech by Peleus to Achilles:

ληγέμεναι δ' ἔριδος κακομηχάνου, ὄφρα σε μᾶλλον
τίωσ' 'Αργείων ἠμὲν νέοι ἠδὲ γέροντες (I 257-258);

the one time it occurs in the *Odyssey*, it modifies Antinoos in the following context:

'Αντίνο', ὕβριν ἔχων κακομήχανε ... (π 418).

Thus the adjective applies to ἔρις, specifically the ἔρις of Achilles which has brought great suffering upon the Achaians, and to Antinoos, who is identified as having ὕβρις which in Homeric language still implies physical violence.[27] Both Achilles and Antinoos represent a threat in their own ways, and so perhaps the danger implied by Helen's reference to herself as a dog is also reflected in her second adjective.

The third modifier, ὀκρυόεις "chilling", appears only once besides this line, in the expression

πολέμου ... ἐπιδημίου ὀκρυόεντος (I 64).

In this passage war is not only chilling, but it is a civil war, a particularly terrible variety of war. Further, the probability that ὀκρυόεις is a misdivision of genitive followed by κρυόεις broadens the possible number of related contexts.[28] κρυόεντος (I 2) mofidies Φόβου,

---

[26] See B. Schlerath, "Der Hund bei den Indogermanen," *Paideuma* 6/1 (1954) 25 ff; also D. Frame, "The Origins of Greek ΝΟΥΣ," Diss. Harvard 1971, pp. 230 f, n. 64. In Indo-European mythology dogs appear to be a threat on the path through the Underworld, prevent souls from getting through the dark to the light on the other side. On this entire theme of mutilation, see Charles Segal, *The Theme of the Mutilation of the Corpse in the Iliad* (Leiden: Brill, 1971).

[27] LSJ s.v. ὕβρις.

[28] See T. B. L. Webster, *From Mycenae to Homer* (New York: Norton, 1964) p. 96.

as the Achaians panic in the face of certain Trojan victory; and Ἰωκή, the personification of Rout worked onto the Aegis (Ε 740), is called κρυόεσσα. The third related word, κρυερός, broadens the implication. At Ν 48 it refers to fear contrasted with warstrength, and its other three occurrences all attach it to grief, γόοιο. Moreover, this grief is specifically that resulting from another's death. Menelaos weeps for the Greeks who died at Troy (δ 103), Odysseus wants to satisfy himself with mourning in the Underworld (λ 212), Achilles urges Priam to check his grief over the dead Hektor (Ω 524). Thus κρυερός and its relatives are all concerned with death, either in the context of panic in the face of violent death on the battlefield or of the chilling grief over someone who has died.

The three modifiers Helen uses for herself, then, are all suggestive of danger and even death. Most colorful is the third, ὀκρυόεις, which actually describes her effect on someone, causing a chilling fear. It happens that several other adjectives surrounding Helen have a similar implication, and indeed every one of her appearances in the epic—in Γ, Ζ, and Ω—contains one such modifier.

The first is at Γ 404, after Helen has recognized Aphrodite and is angrily refusing to rejoin Alexander in his bedchamber:

οὕνεκα δὴ νῦν δῖον Ἀλέξανδρον Μενέλαος
νικήσας ἐθέλει στυγερὴν ἐμὲ οἴκαδ' ἄγεσθαι,
τοὔνεκα δὴ νῦν δεῦρο δολοφρονέουσα παρέστης;
ἧσο παρ' αὐτὸν ἰοῦσα ... (Γ 403-406).

Again she applies a striking epithet to herself, this time στυγερή. Etymologically this word is derived from the root *stug- "to be stiff," which is reflected also in the verb στυγέω "to fear, shrink from the sight of" and the noun στύξ "cold, frost, hate." The latter form is also the familiar Styx, dread river of the Underworld.[29] Now, although the form στύξ, στυγός does exist with the meaning "hate, fear cold," in Homer it appears only as the proper name Στύξ. Moreover,

---

[29] H. Frisk, *Griechisches Etymologisches Wörterbuch* (Heidelberg: Carl Winter, 1960), s.v. στυγέω. Also E. Boisacq, *Dictionnaire étymologique de la langue grecque* (Heidelberg: Carl Winter, 1923), p. 92; also *Et. Mag.* s.v. στυγερός, giving a less scientific explanation of the relationship between cold and fear or hate:

ἐκ τοῦ στυγῶ, τοῦ σημαίνοντος τὸ φοβοῦμαι καὶ τὸ μισῶ, τοῦτο ἐκ τοῦ Στυγός, ἥτις ψυχρότατον ὕδωρ ἔχει. καὶ τί μετέχει τὸ στυγῶ πρὸς τὸ στυγός; μυθεύονται οἱ ἀρχαῖοι, ὅτι τὰ μὲν ἀηδῆ καὶ λυπηρὰ ἐκ τῶν ψυχρῶν καθέστηκε, τὰ ἡδέα καὶ τερπνὰ ἐκ τῶν θερμῶν ...

a survey of the contexts where other Homeric formations on the root appear reveals that the root is invariably associated with death.[30]

---

[30] The possibility remains, however, that the root of the adjective στυγερός may not include the death-connotation of the same root in Στύξ, so it is necessary to survey the contexts of other forms built on the same root. There are seven uses of the verb στυγέω in the *Iliad*, three in the *Odyssey*. Four of the instances are directly concerned with death: Odysseus' men ἔστυγον the Laistrygonian woman just as she is about to make a man her dinner (κ 113); Achilles threatens any who stand in the way of his son,

τῷ κέ τεῳ στύξαιμι μένος καὶ χεῖρας ἀάπτους,
οἵ κεῖνον βιόωνται ἐέργουσίν τ' ἀπὸ τιμῆς,

as he talks to Odysseus in Hades (λ 502 f); Poseidon shakes the earth so violently that Hades himself fears the realms of the dead will be revealed:

ἔδεισεν δ' ὑπένερθεν ἄναξ ἐνέρων Ἀϊδωνεύς,
δείσας δ' ἐκ θρόνου ἆλτο καὶ ἴαχε, μή οἱ ὕπερθε
γαῖαν ἀναρρήξειε Ποσειδάων ἐνοσίχθων,
οἰκία δὲ θνητοῖσι καὶ ἀθανάτοισι φανείη
σμερδαλέ' εὐρώεντα, τά τε στυγέουσι θεοί περ·
τόσσος ἄρα κτύπος ὦρτο θεῶν ἔριδι ξυνιόντων (Υ 61-66).

Perhaps the most striking of these examples comes as Athena speaks to Hera in the *Iliad*:

εἰ γὰρ ἐγὼ τάδε ᾔδε' ἐνὶ φρεσὶ πευκαλίμῃσιν,
εὖτέ μιν εἰς Ἀΐδαο πυλάρταο προὔπεμψεν
ἐξ Ἐρέβευς ἄξοντα κύνα στυγεροῦ Ἀΐδαο,
οὐκ ἂν ὑπεξέφυγε Στυγὸς ὕδατος αἰπὰ ῥέεθρα.
νῦν δ' ἐμὲ μὲν στυγέει, Θέτιδος δ' ἐξήνυσε βουλάς (Θ 366-370).

In all four examples death is not subject or object of the verb, but rather is the context of the verb. Particularly in the last example, the poet clearly has the root * stug- linked in his mind and in his tradition with death, for different forms of it are used three times in a context permeated with death. Nevertheless, one could object that death is logically a situation or fact that would cause one to become stiff with fear; it is necessary to consider less obvious contexts to support the point.

The next large group of contexts for στυγέω refers to or is connected with war and strife. Hektor, as he marshals the Trojans, speaks of someone "fearing" to bring war against Troy (Θ 515 f). Fighting against Hektor is the context of Agamemnon's use of the word (H 111 f), and Agamemnon and Zeus use the verb similarly in references to strife between themselves and their companions (A 186 f, O 160 ff, O 183). The situations seem frequently to contain the notion of someone attacking or fighting with one greater than himself, and such a notion may be part of the link between the death-contexts and war-contexts. The much more obvious link, of course, lies in the fact that death is the result of war, strife, or violence.

The one use of the verb which seems not to fit the pattern so well is at ν 399 f, where Athena is disguising Odysseus for his appearance at the court in Ithaca. She turns him into an older man, a beggar,

... ἀμφὶ δὲ λαῖφος
ἕσσω ὅ κε στυγέῃσιν ἰδὼν ἄνθρωπος ἔχοντα.

In the last book of the *Iliad*, at the end of her lament for Hektor, Helen makes another similar statement:

τῶ σέ θ' ἅμα κλαίω καὶ ἔμ' ἄμμορον ἀχνυμένη κῆρ·
οὐ γάρ τίς μοι ἔτ' ἄλλος ἐνὶ Τροίῃ εὐρείῃ
ἤπιος οὐδὲ φίλος, πάντες δέ με πεφρίκασιν (Ω 773-775).

Φρίσσω is another verb for shuddering, specifically "to bristle, shiver with fear." In Homer there is one instance of the purely agricultural image of bristling grain, ... ὅτε φρίσσουσιν ἄρουραι (Ψ 599). Other contexts are either battle or the hunt: the Trojans shudder at Diomedes as goats at a lion (Λ 383); the boar who gores Odysseus bristles while his eyes flash with fire (τ 446); in a simile, another boar bristles as he confronts hunters approaching (Ν 473); battle bristles with spears (Ν 339); and battle-lines (φάλαγγες and στίχες) bristle σάκεσίν τε καὶ ἔγχεσι ... or ἀσπίσι καὶ κορύθεσσι καὶ ἔγχεσι (Δ 280 ff, Η 61 f).

Again, the contexts are at least violent and sometimes directly connected with warfare. In the two instances where the verb takes a direct object—and the verb appears in the same form in both—one concerns the great warrior Diomedes, the other Helen. Certainly

---

There appears to be no reference to violence here, although Odysseus' disguise will prompt some outrage in the future (e.g. σ 1 ff, 320 ff). What does seem explicit is the reference to old age, another means of approaching death. Indeed, in the *Odyssey*—which concerns the journey of a man who is fated to die at an old age as contrasted with the *Iliad*, where a violent death is commonplace and the end elected by its hero—the notion of old age leading to death is not out of place. Thus all the uses of στυγέω reflect fear or loathing, but that which is ultimately to be feared or loathed is death, brought on by violence or old age.

The adjective στυγερός closely parallels the force of the verb στυγέω. In like fashion, of the forty times the adjective appears in Homer, it is twenty-eight times explicitly connected with death, both through direct means such as fighting (e.g. Ε 47, ξ 235) and indirect means such as disease (e.g. Ν 670); it is five times connected with the warfare that leads to death (e.g. Δ 240); three times it is used for the violent marriage threatening Penelope (α 249, π 126, σ 272 f); once it refers to Hera's attitude toward Zeus as she sees him on Ida during the great battle (Ξ 158); once it is the epithet of the κλαυθμός which Penelope is raising for the absent Telemachos back at the palace (ρ 8); once, problematically, it is the epithet of γαστήρ, than which nothing is κύντερον (η 216). The adverb στυγερῶς is used twice (φ 374, ψ 23) and both times refers to one person violently evicting another from a certain setting. The last situation where the word is used concerns Helen herself, the prize of the contest between Paris and Menelaos. The word certainly can be taken to mean "hateful" here, but it is a special kind of hatred that is evoked— the loathing and fear of Helen, the cause of death through military violence.

Helen is the one reference that does not immediately fit the pattern, unless she is taken as a character more closely identified with war and violence than would seem obvious on the surface from her lament over Hektor.

Thus in each of the three of Helen's appearances in the *Iliad* she is at some point described as a being to be abhorred—she makes people grow stiff or cold with fear (ὀκρυόεσσα and στυγερή) or makes them shiver with fear (φρίσσω). One more word, not used by Helen of herself, but by Achilles describing her, broadens the image. As he mourns Patroklos he remembers the reason for his coming to Troy:

... ὁ δ' ἀλλοδαπῷ ἐνὶ δήμῳ
εἵνεκα ῥιγεδανῆς Ἑλένης Τρωσὶν πολεμίζω (Τ 324-325).

This adjective is used only once in Homer, but other forms of the root do occur—the noun ῥῖγος "cold" (ε 472), comparative adjective ῥίγιον (ρ 191; υ 220; Α 325, 563; Λ 405), superlative ῥίγιστα (Ε 873), and the verb ῥιγέω. Again, the contexts wherein the various forms occur fall into a pattern: the root seems to imply shuddering from fear of death through warfare, or fear of the gods, or fear of the consequences of a violation of trust.[31] In the case of Helen, of course,

---

[31] Of the seven times the noun or adjective appears, only twice does it really refer to temperature (ε 472, ρ 191); all the other times it is best translated "worse" or "worst," and of these twice it refers to the threat of violence —Agamemnon's threat to Achilles (Α 325) and Zeus' to Hera (Α 563)—twice it refers to the gods (Α 563, Ε 873), once it refers to war (Λ 405).
The uses of the verb ῥιγέω can be divided between war-contexts, divinity-contexts, and Helen-contexts. Only once does it mean simply "be cold," when it is conjugated from ῥιγόω (ξ 481). All other places it is conjugated from ῥιγέω. Frequently one warrior will shudder at the sight of the foe advancing, or even at the thought of war (e.g. Μ 331), or at the effects of war (Δ 148, 150; Λ 254). Gods shudder at one another (Kalypso at Hermes' report of Zeus' orders ε 116, Hera at Zeus' threats Ο 34) and man shudders at the gods or tokens of the gods (Odysseus at Kalypso's repetition of Hermes' words ε 171, the Trojans at the omen of a snake dropped by a bird Μ 208, Ajax at his recognition of the gods' work in Hektor's fighting Π 119). Perhaps reflecting the divine contexts, goatherds in a simile shudder before a storm (Δ 279).
The two other Helen-contexts both concern deceit, the betrayal of guest-friend relationships. As Menelaos is about to let fly his weapon in the duel with Alexander, he prays:

Ζεῦ ἄνα, δὸς τείσασθαι ὅ με πρότερος κάκ' ἔοργε,
δῖον Ἀλέξανδρον, καὶ ἐμῆς ὑπὸ χερσὶ δάμασσον,
ὄφρα τις ἐρρίγῃσι καὶ ὀψιγόνων ἀνθρώπων
ξεινοδόκον κακὰ ῥέξαι, ὅ κεν φιλότητα παράσχῃ (Γ 351-354).

Helen is not mentioned directly, but her liaison with Paris is the reason for

all these contexts converge: she, along with Paris, is the example of betrayal of trust, this betrayal is the cause of the war at hand, and behind the motivation for the entire action sit the gods.

In sum, then, lest the audience forget that Helen is the cause and even the living symbol of a terrible war, Homer has used numerous dictional elements in reference to her which make the relationship explicit. Some of them seem to connect her directly with death and violence, some with an undefined danger, some with the effect any danger can have on man—chilling fear. Although Helen is certainly Homer's personification of the Cause of War and as such must be connected with some manner of danger, it is curious that the poet stresses the point so often in such a way. He must be rounding out her character to provide a fuller symbol of the goal of the War. Helen's position in the *Iliad*, then, is a representation of many of the aspects of that goal: the goal is beautiful, but at the same time almost unreal, as the scene with Paris demonstrates; even beyond its ephemeral quality it is terrible, threatening those who fight for it with violent death.

---

the duel, and the background to the speech of Menelaos. Similarly, Penelope mentions Helen as she explains to Odysseus why she did not embrace him immediately:

αὐτὰρ' μὴ νῦν μοι τόδε χώεο μηδὲ νεμέσσα,
οὕνεκά σ' οὐ τὸ πρῶτον, ἐπεὶ ἴδον, ὧδ' ἀγάπησα.
αἰεὶ γάρ μοι θυμὸς ἐνὶ στήθεσσι φίλοισιν
ἐρρίγει μή τίς με βροτῶν ἀπάφοιτο ἔπεσσιν
ἐλθών· πολλοὶ γὰρ κακὰ κέρδεα βουλεύουσιν.
οὐδέ κεν Ἀργείη Ἑλένη, Διὸς ἐκγεγαυῖα,
ἀνδρὶ παρ' ἀλλοδαπῷ ἐμίγη φιλότητι καὶ εὐνῇ,
εἰ ᾔδη ὅ μιν αὖτις ἀρήϊοι υἷες Ἀχαιῶν
ἀξέμεναι οἴκόνδε φίλην ἐς πατρίδ' ἔμελλον (ψ 213-221).

Here Helen is the symbol of the violation of trust. What the tradition seems to be saying is that betrayal of the guest-friend relationship is as horrifying as war or as terrible as the gods.

It should be noted, furthermore, that in the continuation of the speech quoted above, Penelope does blame the gods for all their misfortunes:

τὴν δ' ἦ τοι ῥέξαι θεὸς ὤρορεν ἔργον ἀεικές·
τὴν δ' ἄτην οὐ πρόσθεν ἑῷ ἐγκάτθετο θυμῷ
λυγρήν, ἐξ ἧς πρῶτα καὶ ἡμέας ἵκετο πένθος (ψ 222-224).

CHAPTER TWO

HELEN IN THE *ODYSSEY*

Telemachos' visit with Menelaos and Helen occupies a structurally prominent position in the *Odyssey*: it is the last episode of the Telemachia until Book o, and the direct predecessor to Odysseus' first appearance in the epic. It stands at the end of a sort of prelude which provides information about the absent lord of Ithaca in preparation for the audience's initial glimpse of him brooding on the shore of Kalypso's island; it also must capture the imagination of the audience effectively enough that when the poet returns to Telemachos eleven books later they will still have a fresh memory of just what the youth has been doing in Sparta.

Accordingly the author of the *Odyssey* has filled his fourth book with vivid images and stories. Moreover, he has had the wisdom to realize that an inexperienced youth will react with more awe to a wonderful scene or action, and so has given his audience the palace of Menelaos as seen through the eyes of the young man Telemachos and his companion Peisistratos. This technique allows the poet to be less inhibited about strongly colored descriptions and to be as detached as he wishes in drawing a man and wife who display some characteristics uncomfortably near to the realm of fairy-tale and even the Greek conception of divinity.

The images begin accumulating from the very start of the book. Telemachos and Peisistratos arrive at a palace that is alive with joy and feasting. Although the wedding guests present at the beginning of δ are ignored thereafter, their presence creates a mood of festivity which is echoed later in the book.[1] The marriage-scene here has the aura of a fairy-tale: the son and daughter of Menelaos are being married at the same time, and the daughter is to wed the son of Achilles—a princess marrying a prince. Moreover, this Hermione is Helen's only child, and she is a rare beauty, for

... εἶδος ἔχε χρυσέης 'Αφροδίτης (δ 14).

Nausikaa, even more obviously a fairy-princess, is described similarly,

[1] See pp. 30 ff.

... Ναυσικάα δὲ θεῶν ἄπο κάλλος ἔχουσα (θ 457),

but Hermione is the only character in Homer who has her beauty specifically from Aphrodite. To be accurate, of course, Hermione should be beautiful because Helen is her mother. The suggestion that her beauty is the gift of Aphrodite may simply be a poetic use of the divine, similar to the idea that Athena makes someone's shaft fly straight (e.g. E 290) [2] even though the goddess herself is not present in the battle-scene. Nevertheless, Helen's connection with Aphrodite was quite overt in the *Iliad*, and the statement here may refer to the same theme. At any rate the reference concerning Hermione enhances the fairy-tale quality of the entire passage.

As Telemachos himself notices, the palace fairly gleams with the festivity. The very walls against which servants prop Telemachos' chariot are παμφανόωντα (δ 42), and the inner palace is described more vividly:

ὥς τε γὰρ ἠελίου αἴγλη πέλεν ἠὲ σελήνης
δῶμα καθ' ὑψερεφὲς Μενελάου κυδαλίμοιο (δ 45-46).

Once the youths have bathed and dressed, they take their places at the side of Menelaos where they are served from a beautiful golden pitcher, a silver lebes, and golden drinking cups (δ 52-58). Telemachos wonders at the brilliant beauty of the place, and suggests that Olympos may look something like this:

φράζεο, Νεστορίδη, τῷ ἐμῷ κεχαρισμένε θυμῷ,
χαλκοῦ τε στεροπὴν κὰδ δώματα ἠχήεντα,
χρυσοῦ τ' ἠλέκτρου τε καὶ ἀργύρου ἠδ' ἐλέφαντος.
Ζηνός που τοιήδε γ' Ὀλυμπίου ἔνδοθεν αὐλή,
ὅσσα τάδ' ἄσπετα πολλά· σέβας μ' ἔχει εἰσορόωντα (δ 71-75).

σέβας properly should be the feeling one has in the presence of divinity,[3] and in the *Odyssey* its use is restricted entirely to the formula σέβας μ' ἔχει εἰσορόωντα. The five contexts of the formula are curious: twice the words are spoken as someone looks at Telemachos, so like his father (γ 123, δ 142), and twice Odysseus utters them as he watches a Phaiakian—first Nausikaa (ζ 161), who reminds him

---

[2] G. M. Calhoun, "The Divine Entourage in Homer," *AJP* 61 (1940) 257-277.

[3] LSJ s.v. σέβας, σέβομαι, σοβέω; also A. Meillet and J. Vendryes, *Traité de Grammaire Comparée des langues classiques*, 3rd ed. (Paris: Librairie Ancienne Honoré Champion, 1960), p. 249.

of a tree in the precinct of Apollo on Delos, and later the dancers in the palace (θ 384). Indeed, the description of Alkinoos' palace (η 81-132) is the only picture in the *Odyssey* of a setting that outdoes that of Menelaos, and the hints are frequent that the Phaiakians are somehow closer to the gods than ordinary men (η 49, 108 ff, 117 ff, 199 ff, etc.). The point need not be carried to an extreme: what is clear is that Homer is using the young man's awe as an opportunity to make a daring comparison, and supports the comparison with the Greek expression for reverence before the divine.

In the face of this brilliance, Menelaos is quick to temper the youth's enthusiasm with the reminder that Zeus' palace is immortal, and the Spartan one merely mortal, though perhaps unequalled among the possessions of mortal men (δ 78-82). This assertion is particularly strong in the light of the fact that Menelaos is never going to die (δ 561-569).[4] The Spartan king insists on a humble aspect to his life which is not entirely justified, and then injects his specific note of melancholy:

ἧος ἐγὼ περὶ κεῖνα πολὺν βίοτον συναγείρων
ἠλώμην, τῆός μοι ἀδελφεὸν ἄλλος ἔπεφνε
λάθρῃ, ἀνωϊστί, δόλῳ οὐλομένης ἀλόχοιο·
ὡς οὔ τοι χαίρων τοῖσδε κτεάτεσσιν ἀνάσσω.
καὶ πατέρων τάδε μέλλετ' ἀκουέμεν, οἵ τινες ὑμῖν
εἰσίν, ἐπεὶ μάλα πολλὰ πάθον, καὶ ἀπώλεσα οἶκον
εὖ μάλα ναιετάοντα, κεχανδότα πολλὰ καὶ ἐσθλά.
ὧν ὄφελον τριτάτην περ ἔχων ἐν δώμασι μοῖραν
ναίειν, οἱ δ' ἄνδρες σόοι ἔμμεναι, οἳ τότ' ὄλοντο
Τροίῃ ἐν εὐρείῃ, ἑκὰς Ἄργεος ἱπποβότοιο.
ἀλλ' ἔμπης πάντας μὲν ὀδυρόμενος καὶ ἀχεύων
πολλάκις ἐν μεγάροισι καθήμενος ἡμετέροισιν
ἄλλοτε μέν τε γόῳ φρένα τέρπομαι, ἄλλοτε δ' αὖτε
παύομαι· αἰψηρὸς δὲ κόρος κρυεροῖο γόοιο (δ 90-103).

Menelaos' response to Telemachos mentions two major reasons why the king is not content with his wealth: his brother Agamemnon was murdered even while he himself was amassing his fortune, and he still retains unhappy memories of Troy, particularly the number of brave men who died there. Menelaos thus touches on two of the major themes in the *Odyssey*, both of which concern the wandering

---

[4] See pp. 39 ff.

hero and his son. From the beginning of the epic, the heroes of the Trojan War fall into two groups—those who came back and those who died at Troy (α 346-355, δ 495 ff, etc.). Odysseus represents the only exception to this grouping, and so when his name comes up the question often follows, to which of the two groups does he belong? The theme is worked out most fully in λ, where the living Odysseus visits the dead heroes in the underworld, himself still in a kind of middle existence between life and death. Thus every mention of the men who died at Troy is a reminder of the start of Odysseus' journey and by extension a reminder that he alone of the great heroes has not completed his journey home.[5]

The other theme Menelaos touches on, the tale of Agamemnon, Klytaimnestra, Aigisthos and Orestes, also pervades the epic. At the council on Olympos which begins the poem, it is the story of Agamemnon that the gods are discussing (α 35 ff); Athena in the guise of Mentor tells of Agamemnon's homecoming in contrast to Odysseus' (γ 232-235); Nestor follows with the whole story, explaining to Telemachos why Menelaos was not at hand to prevent his brother's murder (γ 255-275); the Old Man of the Sea tells Aigisthos' plot in a progression from the tale of Ajax, who died at sea, through Agamemnon, who died as he touched land, to Odysseus, who is still wandering (δ 495-560); in the underworld, Agamemnon himself tells Odysseus his fate, ending thus:

ὡς οὐκ αἰνότερον καὶ κύντερον ἄλλο γυναικὸς
ἥ τις δὴ τοιαῦτα μετὰ φρεσὶν ἔργα βάληται·
οἷον δὴ καὶ κείνη ἐμήσατο ἔργον ἀεικές,
κουριδίῳ τεύξασα πόσει φόνον. ἦ τοι ἔφην γε
ἀσπάσιος παίδεσσιν ἰδὲ δμώεσσιν ἐμοῖσιν
οἴκαδ' ἐλεύσεσθαι· ἡ δ' ἔξοχα λυγρὰ ἰδυῖα
οἷ τε κατ' αἶσχος ἔχευε καὶ ἐσσομένῃσιν ὀπίσσω
θηλυτέρῃσι γυναιξί, καὶ ἥ κ' εὐεργὸς ἔῃσιν (λ 427-434).

Odysseus replies:

ὦ πόποι, ἦ μάλα δὴ γόνον Ἀτρέος εὐρύοπα Ζεὺς
ἐκπάγλως ἔχθαιρε γυναικείας διὰ βουλὰς
ἐξ ἀρχῆς· Ἑλένης μὲν ἀπωλόμεθ' εἵνεκα πολλοί,
σοὶ δὲ Κλυταιμνήστρη δόλον ἤρτυε τηλόθ' ἐόντι (λ 436-439).

---

[5] On the entire theme of homecoming, see D. Frame, *passim*.

Agamemnon's last line must remind the audience of Penelope, a wife who is εὐεργός in all respects, and in his answer to Odysseus he draws the proper contrast between himself and the wanderer: Odysseus will have no such threat to face on his return home, for Penelope is ever-faithful and virtuous (λ 444-446). Again, as he speaks to Athena on his arrival on Ithaca, Odysseus reacts to her advice with a reflection on Agamemnon (ν 383-385); and the shade of Agamemnon, speaking with the shade of Amphimedon after Odysseus has slaughtered all the suitors, brings up the subject one more time:

ὄλβιε Λαέρταο πάϊ, πολυμήχαν' Ὀδυσσεῦ,
ἦ ἄρα σὺν μεγάλῃ ἀρετῇ ἐκτήσω ἄκοιτιν·
ὡς ἀγαθαὶ φρένες ἦσαν ἀμύμονι Πηνελοπείῃ,
κούρῃ Ἰκαρίου· ὡς εὖ μέμνητ' Ὀδυσῆος,
ἀνδρὸς κουριδίου. τῷ οἱ κλέος οὔ ποτ' ὀλεῖται
ἧς ἀρετῆς, τεύξουσι δ' ἐπιχθονίοισιν ἀοιδὴν
ἀθάνατοι χαρίεσσαν ἐχέφρονι Πηνελοπείῃ,
οὐχ ὡς Τυνδαρέου κούρη κακὰ μήσατο ἔργα,
κουρίδιον κτείνασα πόσιν, στυγερὴ δέ τ' ἀοιδὴ
ἔσσετ' ἐπ' ἀνθρώπους, χαλεπὴν δέ τε φῆμιν ὀπάσσει
θηλυτέρῃσι γυναιξί, καὶ ἥ κ' εὐεργὸς ἔῃσιν (ω 192-202).

The *Odyssey* clearly considers the tale of Agamemnon important in the working of its main action, the return of Odysseus to Ithaca. Indeed, the story offers some valuable contrast: Odysseus will return home and slay the uninvited suitors, but Agamemnon's uninvited Aigisthos slays him; Penelope faithfully refuses the suitors' advances, but Klytaimnestra succumbs; Agamemnon's son, Orestes, returns to avenge his father's death, but Telemachos and Odysseus will fight the suitors side by side.

Menelaos' response to Telemachos, then, draws in threads from themes which appear throughout the epic. His answer is a melancholy touch, but its implications are much broader than simply to show how unhappy with his lot the hero is. Most curiously, his mention of Agamemnon also involves Helen, Menelaos' queen and certainly part of his unequalled wealth.[6] Not only is Agamemnon the brother of Menelaos, after all, but Klytaimnestra is Helen's sister. Odysseus has properly linked the two ladies in his response to

---
[6] J. Th. Kakridis, "Helena und Odysseus," *Serta Philologica Aenipontana* (Innsbrucker Beiträge zur Kulturwissenschaft) 7/8 (1962) 30 ff.

the shade of Agamemnon (λ 438-439): many died for Helen's sake, and Klytaimnestra killed her husband. Surely the gods must despise the House of Atreus! Even in her role of Cause of War, Helen is associated with Agamemnon. Eumaios speaks of his absent lord, and ends with a curse on Helen:

... ὡς ὤφελλ' Ἑλένης ἀπὸ φῦλον ὀλέσθαι
πρόχνυ, ἐπεὶ πολλῶν ἀνδρῶν ὑπὸ γούνατ' ἔλυσε·
καὶ γὰρ κεῖνος ἔβη Ἀγαμέμνονος εἵνεκα τιμῆς
Ἴλιον εἰς εὔπωλον, ἵνα Τρώεσσι μάχοιτο (ξ 68-71).

A short time later Odysseus in his disguise refers again to the war as being

... Ἀγαμέμνονος εἵνεκα τιμῆς (ξ 117).

Thus mention of Agamemnon or Helen may remind the audience of the rest of the family, collectively responsible for the Trojan War and individually plagued by difficult marriage relationships.

Menelaos' speech to Telemachos ends with a reference to the lost Odysseus, arousing Telemachos to tears (δ 104-116). Menelaos observes him crying, and just as he is wondering whether to question Telemachos about his father, Helen makes her entrance. The setting into which she comes has been described as brilliant, but Menelaos has introduced a note of melancholy—reflected now in Telemachos' weeping—which has muted the colors. Helen is once again pictured in brilliant terms, recalling the initial impression the youths had of the palace, for she is herself compared to an Olympian:

ἤλυθεν Ἀρτέμιδι χρυσηλακάτῳ ἐϊκυῖα (δ 122).

Her servant Phylo brings her an ἀργύρεον τάλαρον (δ 125), which she received from the wife of Egyptian Polybos, who had presented Menelaos with

... δύ' ἀργυρέας ἀσαμίνθους,
δοιοὺς δὲ τρίποδας, δέκα δὲ χρυσοῖο τάλαντα (δ 128-129).

The basket has wheels and an edge of gold, and with it comes a golden distaff reminiscent of Artemis' above (δ 131-132). Helen is likened to the goddess, then, through simile and through the general brilliance which surrounds her, but also represents the perfectly loyal wife with her homely attributes of spinning.[7] She is a queen

---

[7] Whitman, p. 118: spinning marks Helen's return to "domestic propriety.'

and the head of a household. After Menelaos' hint of sadness, she appears to right the picture again with her glorious beauty and wifely stability.

The brilliance of Helen's entrance has contrasted markedly with the tears that immediately preceded it. Now she picks up the theme of Odysseus before Menelaos can say a word, remarking how like Telemachos this young man looks, although she could not have seen him since he was a small child (δ 138-144). She displays here her uncanny power of recognition, which seems similar to her naming of the heroes in *Iliad* Γ [8] and which appears again in Menelaos' tale of how she imitated the voices of the Achaians' wives (δ 277-279). In the midst of all these demonstrations of positive sides to her character, however, Helen cannot resist ending her recognition speech with these words:

... ὅτ' ἐμεῖο κυνώπιδος εἵνεκ' Ἀχαιοὶ
ἤλθεθ' ὑπὸ Τροίην, πόλεμον θρασὺν ὁρμαίνοντες (δ 145 f).

This is a statement from the dark side of Helen, the Helen who brought about the Trojan War and seems to recognize her own unworthiness. So once again the seeming beauty of a moment—or, as here, of a person—is undercut by a less explicit, negative aspect.

Menelaos picks up the conversation; they speak of Odysseus and begin to weep again. At this point an incident occurs which will shed some light on the Homeric character of Menelaos. In order to deal with the incident adequately, it is best to begin by considering Megapenthes, the son of Menelaos by a slave-woman (δ 11-12).

In epic tradition, the name of a hero's son frequently refers to a characteristic of the father and has in fact nothing to do with the son. For example, Astyanax is so named because *Hektor* is lord of the city (Z 403); Telemachos may refer to Odysseus' distance from home or perhaps his prowess as an archer; Peisistratos clearly represents Nestor's position among the Argive troops, not the youth's. Accordingly the name Megapenthes may refer to a characteristic of Menelaos. There is no other character in Homer whose name contains the πένθος element, but the collocation μέγα ... πένθος is quite common, occurring in seven instances where sorrow overcomes someone.[9] The opposite to πένθος is κλέος, as Gregory Nagy has shown in

---
[8] See pp. 9 ff.
[9] A 254, Δ 416 f, H 124, P 138 f, λ 195, ρ 489, ω 232 f.

his consideration of the phrase, κλέος ἄφθιτον,[10] and it is a Homeric understanding that a hero who wins a contest receives κλέος, but the one who loses receives only πένθος. As Phemios sings the νόστοι of the Achaians, Penelope reacts negatively, saying the subject is a πένθος ἄλαστον for her (α 342), since her hero-husband has not returned. When Menelaos has been wounded following his abbreviated duel with Paris, Agamemnon says that his misfortune is a κλέος for the archer who shot him, but a πένθος for the Achaians:

... τῷ μὲν κλέος, ἄμμι δὲ πένθος (Δ 197 = 207).

It is curious, therefore, that the hero who has won and retrieved his wife should be characterized by πένθος. Menelaos has just cause to be sorrowful in the *Iliad*, when he reflects on the suffering that his quest for Helen has brought upon the Achaians:

... μάλιστα γὰρ ἄλγος ἱκάνει
θυμὸν ἐμόν, φρονέω δὲ διακρινθήμεναι ἤδη
Ἀργείους καὶ Τρῶας, ἐπεὶ κακὰ πολλὰ πέπασθε
εἵνεκ' ἐμῆς ἔριδος καὶ Ἀλεξάνδρου ἕνεκ' ἀρχῆς (Γ 97-100).

But the war is over now, and although the hero can remember the suffering, he should not be so profoundly dominated by πένθος as the name of his son would indicate. One might argue that the name refers only to a period of time when Menelaos was bereft of Helen, but study of the names of other sons indicates that in fact they denote a constant in the fathers.[11] If, on the other hand, Menelaos had a πένθος ἄλαστον, a case might be made for the idea that even once he retrieved his wife, he still retained his former grief. It is noteworthy that all the figures who have πένθος ἄλαστον have lost someone close to them: Penelope has lost Odysseus (α 342), Eupeithes his son Antinoos (ω 423), Thetis has figuratively lost Achilles with the death of Hektor (Ω 105), Tros has lost Ganymede (*H. Ven.* 207). Although Menelaos does not have πένθος ἄλαστον, he does have ἄχος ἄλαστον the only time the collocation occurs in Homer:

... ἐμοὶ δ' ἄχος αἰὲν ἄλαστον
κείνου, ὅπως δὴ δηρὸν ἀποίχεται, οὐδέ τι ἴδμεν,
ζώει ὅ γ' ἢ τέθνηκεν (δ 108-110).

---

[10] G. Nagy, p. 255.
[11] E.g., Orestes' son, Teisomenos "Avenger" (Apollodorus II. 176); Eurysakes reminds us that Ajax is above all the mighty bulwark with a shield like a tower (Soph. *Ajax, passim*).

His ἄχος, however, is not for his lost wife but rather for the lost Odysseus. This would be the only case in Homer where someone has πένθος/ἄχος ἄλαστον because of a comrade rather than kin. The traditional thematic evidence, then, points to the idea that his ἄχος probably was really for Helen, and had been transferred to Odysseus for the immediate context of the *Odyssey*. A further implication is that the basic characterization of Menelaos is as the man who has lost his wife—for in fact the most important thing Menelaos ever did for epic was to lose Helen in the first place. Thus his real character is that of the bereft husband, and it is impossible for him to escape that character in the context of the *Odyssey*. His ἄχος for Odysseus is one indication of his real character, and the name of his son another. Furthermore, as was mentioned above,[12] there is evidence in the very action of the *Odyssey* that πένθος still sits heavily on the Spartan hero.

Not only is κλέος the opposite to πένθος, but Hesiod clearly tells us that it is an antidote for it:

εἰ γάρ τις καὶ πένθος ἔχων νεοκηδέι θυμῷ
ἄζηται κραδίην ἀκαχήμενος, αὐτὰρ ἀοιδὸς
Μουσάων θεράπων κλέεα προτέρων ἀνθρώπων
ὑμνήσῃ μάκαράς τε θεούς, οἳ Ὄλυμπον ἔχουσιν,
αἶψ' ὅ γε δυσφροσυνέων ἐπιλήθεται οὐδέ τι κηδέων
μέμνηται· ταχέως δὲ παρέτραπε δῶρα θεάων (*Theogony* 98-103).

In fact, Achilles applies this antidote to himself at I 185-191 where he relieves his sorrow by singing κλέα ἀνδρῶν. In Telemachos' encounter with Menelaos, old πένθος has been reawakened, and now Helen acts to relieve it. Into the wine they are drinking she mixes the drug

νηπενθές τ' ἄχολόν τε, κακῶν ἐπίληθον ἁπάντων.
ὃς τὸ καταβρόξειεν, ἐπεὶ κρητῆρι μιγείη,
οὔ κεν ἐφημέριός γε βάλοι κατὰ δάκρυ παρειῶν,
οὐδ' εἴ οἱ κατατεθναίη μήτηρ τε πατήρ τε,
οὐδ' εἴ οἱ προπάροιθεν ἀδελφεὸν ἢ φίλον υἱὸν
χαλκῷ δηιόωεν, ὁ δ' ὀφθαλμοῖσιν ὁρῷτο (δ 221-226).

The incident seems to hint at witch-like powers for Helen, although the poet is quick to state that she procured the brew from her

---

[12] See pp. 26 ff.

Egyptian friend Polydamna. The brew appears to be quite exotic, and even in terms of Homeric diction it is a rarity, for νηπενθές, ἄχολον, and ἐπίληθον all occur only here in Homer. It is not clear what the tradition may be for the hapax line itself, but from the standpoint of the larger passage it serves as an explicit reference to what the action contains implicitly: Helen removes the πένθος of the moment with means whose vocabulary suggests epic poetry! Even the drug's epithets recall Hesiod's statement: the drug is anti-πένθος, and brings forgetfulness, ἐπίληθον (δ 221) vs. ἐπιλήθεται (*Theogony* 102). As soon as the drugged wine has been offered to those present, Helen acts as a poet by entertaining the company with a lengthy tale of herself and Odysseus:

ἦ τοι νῦν δαίνυσθε· καθήμενοι ἐν μεγάροισι
καὶ μύθοις τέρπεσθε· ἐοικότα γὰρ καταλέξω (δ 238-239).[13]

Thus the brew, νηπενθές, anti-πένθος, may be seen as a brief symbol for Homer's extended self-conscious expression of the effect of epic poetry. Within the context of the action, moreover, it provides another example of a theme that is beginning to emerge: the entire household of Menelaos appears to be rich and happy, but the appearance is hollow, masking a deeper sorrow. Helen covers the πένθος with her drug and the real antidote of epic poetry, but from the name of Megapenthes there remains an unsettling suggestion that the πένθος will return.[14]

Helen tells a story that places her in a good light. As Odysseus, disguised as a beggar, enters Troy, Helen alone recognizes him (δ 250) and cares for him herself. She swears she will not betray him (δ 253-5) and he tells her the plans of the Greeks and escapes again, having slaughtered a few Trojans along the way (δ 256-258). Now Helen adds:

---

[13] With reference to the entire section following, L. Muellner has noted that Helen's entrance at δ 120 and her words at 140 should thematically imply that she is behaving as a Muse. The introductory line

ἧος ὁ ταῦθ' ὅρμαινε κατὰ φρένα καὶ κατὰ θυμόν (120)

elsewhere signals the appearance of a god—Athena (A 193 and ε 424) and Poseidon (ε 365); Helen's expression ψεύσομαι, ἢ ἔτυμον ἐρέω (140) recalls the song of the Muses in Hesiod:

ἴδμεν ψεύδεα πολλὰ λέγειν ἐτύμοισιν ὁμοῖα,
ἴδμεν δ' εὖτ' ἐθέλωμεν, ἀληθέα γηρύσασθαι (*Theog.*, 27-28).

[14] On this entire episode, see also W. S. Anderson, "Calypso and Elysium," *Classical Journal* 54 (1958) pp. 2-11, and E. A. S. Butterworth, *Some Traces of the Pre-Olympian World* (Berlin: de Gruyter, 1966), p. 175.

ἔνθ' ἄλλαι Τρῳαὶ λίγ' ἐκώκυον· αὐτὰρ ἐμὸν κῆρ
χαῖρ', ἐπεὶ ἤδη μοι κραδίη τέτραπτο νέεσθαι
ἄψ οἶκόνδ', ἄτην δὲ μετέστενον, ἣν Ἀφροδίτη
δῶχ', ὅτε μ' ἤγαγε κεῖσε φίλης ἀπὸ πατρίδος αἴης,
παῖδά τ' ἐμὴν νοσφισσαμένην θάλαμόν τε πόσιν τε
οὔ τευ δευόμενον, οὔτ' ἄρ φρένας οὔτε τι εἶδος (δ 259-264).

She pictures herself as a loyal Greek, anxious to be of help to the Achaian cause, specifically friendly to Odysseus, and once again faithful to her former husband, who lacks nothing.

Now Menelaos takes up the storytelling, and in the course of his tale undercuts what Helen has tried to demonstrate. He creates another scene between Helen and Odysseus, chronologically later than Helen's story, when Odysseus was inside the Horse with the Achaians and Helen was outside, trying to trick them into betraying themselves (δ 277-279). Not only does this story disagree with Helen's assertion of loyalty to the Greek cause, but it also demonstrates her own fickleness, for she appears in the scene with Deiphobos, her third husband:

... κελευσέμεναι δέ σ' ἔμελλε
δαίμων, ὃς Τρώεσσιν ἐβούλετο κῦδος ὀρέξαι·
καί τοι Δηίφοβος θεοείκελος ἕσπετ' ἰούσῃ (δ 274-276).

Menelaos tries to fault the gods for Helen's action, but in the same breath adds another piece of evidence against her fidelity. Furthermore, he expands on her witchlike character with his description of how she imitated the voices of the heroes' wives. How did she know the voices of these women? Or *which* Achaians' wives to imitate? Or that there were Achaians inside at all? A good deal of ink has been spilled on this problem,[15] but the only available answer is that Helen has special powers of insight and expression.

It has been suggested [16] that the inconsistent accounts of Helen and Menelaos represent their way of coping with pent-up resentments they have held since the Trojan War. Certainly in part Homer may be dealing with the question of how this pair might behave after the War is over, when they are back to their peaceful Spartan existence. It is important to remember, nevertheless, that Homer

---

[15] E.g., Kakridis, "Helena und Odysseus," *passim*.
[16] C. R. Beye, *The Iliad, the Odyssey, and the Epic Tradition* (Garden City: Doubleday, 1966), pp. 173 f.

may be using existing traditional material from perhaps at least two different ways of telling Helen's story: in one she is loyal to the Greeks, in the other to the Trojans.[17] Homer tells the two versions without comment, but he places the disloyal Helen in the second, stronger narrative position. The audience is naturally left believing the second account to be the more accurate, and Helen to be less credible than her spouse. There also remains the lingering suggestion that a story strongly identified with the drug that artificially removes all one's sorrows may be in some sense artificial, as well. So a possible tension between the married couple could well be a major part of Homer's purpose in this scene; in a larger sense, it is one more example of a glorious illusion shattered by a less-than-glorious reality.

The rest of the scene is concerned with Menelaos' νόστος, and Helen as a character does not re-enter until o 104 ff, where she chooses out a peplos for Telemachos that she herself has made. She gives it to Telemachos and bids him give it to Penelope to save for his bride on their wedding day. The theme of marriage, suggested by Menelaos' earlier mention of Agamemnon and Klytaimnestra, and treated at length in the whole scene between Helen and Menelaos in δ, has now been projected into the future. Penelope herself, whose relationship with Odysseus must be the ultimate kernel of Homer's working of the theme, appears as the temporary recipient of the robe. As Helen mentions her, the audience may recall for a moment the position of Penelope regarding marriage: her lord is still away, the uninvited suitors urge her to choose one, and she is under pressure from her brothers and father to marry (o 16 f).

Helen's reference, then, makes the logical contrast between herself and Penelope more explicit for the moment. Penelope recalls the contrast much later, significantly in the speech where she explains to Odysseus why she did not embrace him immediately:

αἰεὶ γάρ μοι θυμὸς ἐνὶ στήθεσσι φίλοισιν
ἐρρίγει μή τίς με βροτῶν ἀπάφοιτο ἔπεσσιν
ἐλθών· πολλοὶ γὰρ κακὰ κέρδεα βουλεύουσιν.
οὐδέ κεν 'Αργείη 'Ελένη, Διὸς ἐκγεγαυῖα,
ἀνδρὶ παρ' ἀλλοδαπῷ ἐμίγη φιλότητι καὶ εὐνῇ,
εἰ ᾔδη ὅ μιν αὖτις ἀρήϊοι υἷες 'Αχαιῶν
ἀξέμεναι οἶκόνδε φίλην ἐς πατρίδ' ἔμελλον.

---

[17] Kakridis, "Helena und Odysseus," *passim*.

τὴν δ' ἥ τοι ῥέξαι θεὸς ὤρορεν ἔργον ἀεικές·
τὴν δ' ἄτην οὐ πρόσθεν ἑῷ ἐγκάτθετο θυμῷ
λυγρήν, ἐξ ἧς πρῶτα καὶ ἡμέας ἵκετο πένθος (ψ 215-224).

Penelope represents Helen as being a victim of the gods, who have laid upon her an ἄτη which causes her to run off with a foreign man. Again, as in the *Iliad*, the major passion manifested in Helen is sexual desire. The phrase φιλότητι καὶ εὐνῇ (ψ 219) means nothing but the act of sexual intercourse, and the same phrase is used by Paris in his proposition to Helen at Γ 445.[18] Now, when Odysseus in disguise tells Penelope of having seen Odysseus in Crete, he includes the following as he begins to reassure her:

ὦ γύναι αἰδοίη Λαερτιάδεω Ὀδυσῆος,
μηκέτι νῦν χρόα καλὸν ἐναίρεο μηδέ τι θυμὸν
τῆκε πόσιν γοόωσα· νεμεσσῶμαί γε μὲν οὐδέν·
καὶ γάρ τις τ' ἀλλοῖον ὀδύρεται ἄνδρ' ὀλέσασα
κουρίδιον, τῷ τέκνα τέκῃ φιλότητι μιγεῖσα,
ἢ Ὀδυσῆ', ὅν φασι θεοῖς ἐναλίγκιον εἶναι (τ 262-267).

This is the closest anyone comes to using φιλότητι καὶ εὐνῇ in a reference to Penelope. Odysseus is uttering a generality, but he is also a disguised husband speaking to his wife, so Homer may wish the audience to hear the word as suggestive of Odysseus' and Penelope's relationship. What is clear is that many of the sexual unions described in the *Odyssey* contain this phrase, but when Odysseus at last stands revealed to his patient wife the tone is quite different. Their relationship is deeper than simply φιλότης καὶ εὐνή; even the lengthy discussion of their marriage bed (ψ 174-204) contains implications that reach far beyond the pleasure of sex. Thus when Penelope speaks of Helen, although she is at pains to justify the lady's action, she also voices one of the great contrasts between the two women: Helen is the plaything of the gods, and the means through

---

[18] In the *Odyssey* it refers to Demeter and Iasion (ε 126), Kirke uses it as she tries to seduce Odysseus (κ 335), and Eumaios mentions it as a factor in the treachery of the Phoenician woman in his father's house (ο 421). The single word φιλότης can refer to a simple friendship (γ 363, χ 43, ξ 505), but more often it serves as a shorter form for the φιλότητι καὶ εὐνῇ expression. The couples involved are for the most part people characterized by sexual desire: Kalypso and Odysseus (ε 277), the lady in part representing some of the same ideas as Helen in the *Iliad*—simple physical pleasure and escape from the real world; Ares and Aphrodite in the Lay of Demodokos (θ 271 and 313), the parody of unfaithfulness and its punishment; Tyro and Poseidon, whose story Odysseus hears in the Underworld (λ 248).

which they ensnare her is desire; Penelope is also a victim of the gods, but she does not give way to any temptation. She is faithful to Odysseus, who represents to her much more than physical pleasure.

The comparison of Penelope with Helen is invited at two more crucial moments in the epic, Helen's interpretation of the bird-sign and Penelope's dream. As Telemachos prepares to leave Sparta, and as Menelaos bids him farewell and pours a libation, an eagle flies by with a goose clutched in its talons (ο 160-165). Peisistratos asks Menelaos to interpret it, and as the latter turns over what the sign may mean, Helen anticipates him and gives the interpretation that Odysseus will come home and destroy the suitors (169-178). Her special powers extend to the understanding of omens, for in fact her interpretation of the sign is correct. Besides this power, however, Helen also demonstrates how imperfect her relationship with Menelaos is, interrupting him as no good wife should. She is taking charge again, as she did upon Telemachos' arrival when she recognized him before Menelaos had a chance to (δ 148 ff), as she did when she drugged the wine (δ 219 ff) and when she instead of her husband began the story-telling (δ 238 ff). The poet is providing one more example of how the glittering marriage of Helen and Menelaos is devoid of real affection.

Penelope's dream, on the other hand, appears in a far different context. After a long interview with the disguised Odysseus (τ 104-360), Penelope tells Eurykleia to bathe his feet, during which time he is made known to the old servant by the sign of his scar. With no reference to what she may or may not have noticed of the exchange between the beggar and servant, Penelope begins to take a new tack in her conversation. Point by point she makes trial of Odysseus, but the time is not yet right for him to reveal himself. She begins by telling him how she lies in her bed anxiously (τ 515-518), wondering whether to go with one of the suitors or remain faithful to Odysseus (τ 525-534). She follows with her famous description of the dream, in which again an eagle kills her geese. The eagle himself, who is really Odysseus, interprets the dream as meaning that her husband is home and will kill the suitors—exactly what Helen had predicted earlier (ο 169-178). Penelope asks the disguised Odysseus what this dream may mean, and he answers that she must believe the dream's own interpretation. She then voices her doubt as to the truth of the dream in the description of the gates of horn and ivory, and finally expresses the belief that her dream came through the ivory gate (τ 560-569). Now begins her final attempt to get Odysseus to reveal himself:

ἄλλο δέ τοι ἐρέω, σὺ δ' ἐνὶ φρεσὶ βάλλεο σῇσιν·
ἥδε δὴ ἠὼς εἶσι δυσώνυμος, ἥ μ' 'Οδυσῆος
οἴκου ἀποσχήσει· νῦν γὰρ καταθήσω ἄεθλον,
τοὺς πελέκεας, τοὺς κεῖνος ἐνὶ μεγάροισιν ἑοῖσιν
ἵστασχ' ἐξείης, δρυόχους ὥς, δώδεκα πάντας·
στὰς δ' ὅ γε πολλὸν ἄνευθε διαρρίπτασκεν ὀιστόν.
νῦν δὲ μνηστήρεσσιν ἄεθλον τοῦτον ἐφήσω·
ὃς δέ κε ῥηΐτατ' ἐντανύσῃ βιὸν ἐν παλάμῃσι
καὶ διοϊστεύσῃ πελέκεων δυοκαίδεκα πάντων,
τῷ κεν ἅμ' ἑσποίμην, νοσφισσαμένη τόδε δῶμα
κουρίδιον, μάλα καλόν, ἐνίπλειον βιότοιο,
τοῦ ποτε μεμνήσεσθαι ὀΐομαι ἔν περ ὀνείρῳ (τ 570-581).

Odysseus answers:

ὦ γύναι αἰδοίη Λαερτιάδεω 'Οδυσῆος,
μηκέτι νῦν ἀνάβαλλε δόμοις ἔνι τοῦτον ἄεθλον·
πρὶν γάρ τοι πολύμητις ἐλεύσεται ἐνθάδ' 'Οδυσσεύς,
πρὶν τούτους τόδε τόξον ἐΰξοον ἀμφαφόωντας
νευρήν τ' ἐντανύσαι διοϊστεῦσαί τε σιδήρου (τ 583-587).

It would be hard for the two of them to be more open about Odysseus' identity, given his decision still to retain his disguise. In a sense this scene is parallel to that of Helen trying to trick the Achaian heroes: Penelope makes statements that might lead Odysseus to betray himself, among them threats to forsake him for another, but he remains resolute, as he did inside the Horse. The motives are different, however; Helen attempts to destroy her husband by betraying him, while Penelope only wants to be assured that he is safe with her. Penelope's entire scene with Odysseus expresses her love for him in various ways: the story of Helen and the Horse, on the other hand, as well as of Helen the omen-reader, expresses her disregard for any authentic love.

The depth of the contrast evoked by these two moments in Book o suggests that one important reason for Helen's presence in the *Odyssey* is to serve as a foil for Penelope. One could certainly argue that every woman in the epic must ultimately be compared with Penelope, and each represents a slightly different type of alternative to the kind of homecoming Odysseus chooses. The differences between many of the ladies and Penelope are obvious—Kirke is a witch, Kalypso an immortal nymph, Nausikaa a princess in a sort of Never-Neverland. Helen is established in Sparta, a place not so far removed from Ithaca, and so Homer must show by less bold means how she ties into the Penelope-scheme.

At each of their appearances in the epic, it has been observed how every beautiful aspect of Helen and Menelaos' life together has its darker side. Homer also takes pains to paint the lady as somewhat exotic, as the references to Egypt exemplify. Tradition clearly knew a version in which Helen and Menelaos—and possibly Paris, as well —visited Egypt,[19] and for the sake of artistic unity the poet of each epic chose not to make extensive use of it. Nevertheless, Homer does refer to this tradition when he tells us of the workbasket Helen received from the Egyptian Alkandre (δ 125 f) and the magic potion she had from the Egyptian Polydamna, wife of Thon (δ 220-229). Furthermore, Menelaos tells of a prolonged stay in Egypt after the War, during which time he wrestled with a sea-god and won from him a prophecy (δ 351-570). The prophecy specifically mentions Helen, and represents Homer's most direct expression of her exotic nature:

σοὶ δ' οὐ θέσφατόν ἐστι, διοτρεφὲς ὦ Μενέλαε,
"Ἄργει ἐν ἱπποβότῳ θανέειν καὶ πότμον ἐπισπεῖν,
ἀλλά σ' ἐς Ἠλύσιον πεδίον καὶ πείρατα γαίης
ἀθάνατοι πέμψουσιν, ὅθι ξανθὸς Ῥαδάμανθυς,
τῇ περ ῥηίστη βιοτὴ πέλει ἀνθρώποισιν·
οὐ νιφετός, οὔτ' ἄρ χειμὼν πολὺς οὔτε ποτ' ὄμβρος,
ἀλλ' αἰεὶ Ζεφύροιο λιγὺ πνείοντος ἀήτας
Ὠκεανὸς ἀνίησιν ἀναψύχειν ἀνθρώπους,
οὕνεκ' ἔχεις Ἑλένην καί σφιν γαμβρὸς Διός ἐσσι (δ 561-569).

This statement approaches a direct reference to Helen's divinity, but Homer (or Proteus) softens it with σφιν in the last line, stating that in the eyes of the *immortals* Menelaos is the son-in-law of Zeus. So it goes with all the near-acknowledgements of her nature: she is the daughter of Zeus, has strange powers of recognition and imitation, knows formulas to banish cares, and can somehow bestow immortality upon her husband, but never is she actually called a

---

[19] Z 289 ff and Herodotus II 116. 1-3.

goddess or even a nymph. It is certain that Homer must be emphasizing Helen's human side for the artistic purposes of the *Odyssey*. By maintaining her humanity, Homer allows himself to fill out his spectrum of heroic marriages. On the one hand he portrays Klytaimnestra and Agamemnon, marked by hatred, violence, and death. On the other he shows us Helen and Menelaos, unhappy although promised immortality. Penelope and Odysseus, certainly, must strike the medium between those extremes. The hero has rejected the life exemplified by Menelaos and Helen in his rejection of Kalypso,[20] and it has been demonstrated how importantly the Agamemnon-Klytaimnestra theme figures in the presentation of Odysseus' and Penelope's contrasting, faithful relationship. Thus, although Homer can allow Helen to be the possessor of uncommon powers, his system of foils for Odysseus and Penelope necessitates that he present her as essentially human.

The Helen who appears in the action of the *Iliad* and the *Odyssey*, then, is a many-faceted character. She can be a positive force, as she portrays herself in her tale of Odysseus in Troy, but she can also be destructive, as in the parallel tale told by Menelaos. She is strongly identified with Aphrodite, and her relationship with that goddess appears to be as dangerous as it is supportive. She comes into contact with the central themes of both epics through her association with poetry: she represents the shining but deadly goal of the Trojan War, and participates in the world of unreality—the world of νηπενθές—from which Odysseus is struggling to emerge. Though terrible to behold, she is attractive not only because of her beauty but also because of her extraordinary powers of recognition and prediction; and although she will be the cause for the poetic immortality of the great heroes and the more literal immortality of her husband, still Menelaos is burdened with a sadness that seems again to have been brought about by Helen. In short, she appears to have a dual nature which is reflected in many of her relationships and activities; if it is true, moreover, that the traditional epic diction is also an important factor in shaping the very action of an epic, this nature of Helen which has emerged from the consideration of epic action should also be manifested in the epithets and themes through which the tradition defines her.

---

[20] See W. S. Anderson, *passim*.

CHAPTER THREE

THE CHARACTER OF HELEN IN EPIC DICTION

The following chart lists the epithets given to Helen in the Homeric epics, and the other characters with she whom shares them. The numerals indicate the frequency of occurrence of the epithet-noun group in each of the two epics, and in the Hymns taken as a whole.

I. Directly attached to her name

	Iliad	*Odyssey*	*Hymns*
A. λευκώλενος			
Helen	1	1	
Hera	24		5
Andromache	3		
Arete		3	
Nausikaa		4	
δμωαί		1	
ἀμφίπολοι		2	
Selene			1
B. τανύπεπλος			
Helen	1	2	
Thetis	2		
Lampetie (nymph)		1	
Ktimene (sister of Odysseus)		1	
C. κούρη Διός or Διὸς κούρη			
Helen	1		
Athena	3	10	1
for Athena		5	
Nymphs	1	4	
Artemis	1	1	
Muses	1		1
Litai	3		
Aphrodite	1		

		Iliad	Odyssey	Hymns
D. Ἀργείη Ἑλένη, Διὸς ἐκγεγαυῖα				
	Helen		2	
E. Διὸς ἐκγεγαυῖα (alone)				
	Helen	2	1	
	Athena		1	
F. Ἀργείη (alone)				
	Helen	9	2	
	Hera	2		
G. ῥιγεδανῆς				
	Helen	1		

II. Separated from her name

A. καλλιπάρῃος

	Iliad	Odyssey	Hymns
Helen		1	
Leto	1		
Chryseis	3		
Briseis	5		
Theano	3		
Diomede	1		
Themis	1		
Melantho		1	

B. Ἀλέξανδρος Ἑλένης πόσις ἠϋκόμοιο

Helen	6		

C. ἠΰκομος

	Iliad	Odyssey	Hymns
Helen	1		
Hera	1		
Briseis	1		
Leto	2	1	3
Niobe	1		
Thetis	2		
Athena	3		
Kalypso		2	
Nymphs			1
Demeter			6
μήτηρ	1		
Rheia			1

		Iliad	*Odyssey*	*Hymns*
D. καλλίκομος				
	Helen		1	
	παλλακίς	1		
E. λευκωλένῳ εὐπατερείῃ				
	Helen	1		
F. εὐπατέρεια (alone)				
	Helen	1		
	Tyro (mother of Pelias and Neleus, lover of Poseidon)		1	
G. δῖα γυναικῶν				
	Helen	2	2	
	Penelope		8	
	Alkestis	1		
	Eurykleia		1	

III. Without Helen's name

		Iliad	*Odyssey*	*Hymns*
A. δῖα γυναικῶν				
	Helen	1		
B. Διὸς θυγάτηρ				
	Helen		1	
	Artemis		1	
	Aphrodite	9	1	4
	Athena	4	5	
	Muse		1	1
	Ate	1		
	Persephone		1	
	Ageleia	1		
C. κυνῶπις				
	Helen	1	1	
	Aphrodite		1	
	Klytaimnestra		1	
	Agamemnon (κυνώπης)	1		
	Hera	1		

D. νύμφα (other than Νύμφαι)	Iliad	Odyssey	Hymns
Helen	1		
Penelope		2	
Kalypso		10	
Thoosa		1	
Kirke		1	
Maia			5
Brides	1		
Abarbare (mother of twins)	1		
Alkyone	1		
E. στυγερή			
Helen	1		

In order to analyze the diction surrounding Helen in Homeric epic, one must decide whether a particular epithet is significant for a given character or whether it should be classified as "generic," the term Parry used for a word that has been employed in so many contexts of the same metrical shape that the word has lost its surface meaning.[1] In the case of Helen the words seem to fall into three groups—those which are truly "generic" and have no special meaning for Helen, those which appear to be specialized in a particular poetic context, and those which seem to say something profound about Helen's traditional nature. The analysis of the diction in this last category naturally leads to a discussion of further dictional motifs surrounding Helen which may shed some light upon her origins.

I

a. λευκώλενος

This epithet appears to be the standard filler between penthemimeral caesura and bucolic dieresis for a female character, since with the exception of the cases where it modifies Hera, it always stands at that one point in the line.[2] None of the ladies besides Hera has another formula for the same gap. Hera does, however, present a problem. Of twenty-seven occurrences of the word in the *Iliad*, twenty-three are connected with her, and she does have an alternate filler: θεὰ λευλώχενος "Ηρη = βοῶπις πότνια "Ηρη.[3] Despite Parry's

---

[1] M. Parry, *The Making of Homeric Verse*, p. 149.
[2] Parry, *The Making of Homeric Verse*, pp. 97 ff.
[3] The one metrical exception is *H. Ap.* 99, where λευκώλενος is in the usual position, modifying Hera.

contention that an epithet is generic once it modifies more than one character,⁴ the overwhelming preponderance of uses with Hera, as well as the fact that in the metrical position λευκώλενος X̄X̆ the word modifies only Hera, certainly points to the view that in some measure λευκώλενος is Hera's particular epithet, borrowed by the poet for other ladies. Thus it could be an overstatement to assert that a lady called λευκώλενος is *not* connected with Hera in any way.

b. τανύπεπλος

In all cases except that of Lampetie, this adjective carries the name-epithet combination to the feminine caesura. It is perhaps noteworthy that except for Helen and Lampetie the adjective describes only nymphs.

c. καλλιπάρῃος, καλλίκομος, εὐπατέρεια, δῖα γυναικῶν

Of the adjectives not directly next to Helen's name, most seem to be what Parry termed generic. It appears that almost any lady may be "fair-cheeked" (καλλιπάρῃος simply fills the gap between bucolic dieresis and end of line) or "fair-haired." It may be significant that the lists of ladies so designated are heavily loaded with goddesses and nymphs, and that Penelope, for instance, is conspicuously absent. εὐπατέρεια is shared by Helen and Tyro, mother of Pelias and Neleus, and lover of Poseidon, but one can hardly guess more than that it is the logical adjective for Helen, a lady whose father is Zeus. δῖα γυναικῶν is another filler for the slot following the bucolic dieresis, and all one can say about it is that it is shared by women of exceptional quality.

d. ἠΰκομος

The only seemingly generic epithet besides δῖα γυναικῶν used often enough for Helen to justify further consideration is ἠΰκομος. Six time it occurs with Helen's name in the pattern

Ἀλέξανδρος Ἑλένης πόσις ἠϋκόμοιο.

There is another πόσις often modified thus:

ἐρίγδουπος πόσις Ἥρης.⁵

---

⁴ Parry, *The Making of Homeric Verse*, pp. 148 ff.
⁵ H 411, K 329, N 154, Π 88, θ 465, o 180, o 112.

Once, moreover, Zeus is described in a line parallel to Alexandros', the only time Hera's name is used with ἠϋκόμοιο:

πόσις "Ηρης ἠϋκόμοιο (κ 5).

The parallel is striking, particularly when one considers the relative importance of the πόσις and his lady; Helen is certainly the stronger figure in her context, and grammatically Zeus, too, loses out to Hera (after all, he is being identified by means of her). The expression would seem to be rooted in a period when Hera was still the earth goddess and Zeus was her consort, or was taking the place of her consort.[6] Can it justifiably be claimed that the Helen expression is equally old? For the moment, a simple acknowledgement of parallelism must suffice.[7]

e. νύμφα

The meaning of this epithet is something of a mystery. Kalypso, who is indeed a nymph, receives this title most often. Helen's instance, however, is in the *Iliad*, where she shares the word only with brides, Abarbare, and Alkyone. Alkyone is the mother of Kleopatra, Meleager's bride; Abarbare is a naiad. Thus the word can denote an actual nymph, or a bride who is traditionally human. What the word may mean in the case of Helen is not clear.

f. κυνῶπις

From the contexts surrounding this word it is clear that it is a term of reproach.[8] Helen also calls herself a dog twice,[9] and that word is used to reproach despicable people no less than eighteen other times in Homer. Thus κυνῶπις may be no more than an insult. Nevertheless, four out of six appearances of the epithet κυνῶπις/κυνώπης refer to members of the house of Atreus, and the two others to the powerful goddesses Hera and Aphrodite. The relationship between the latter goddess and Helen has been explored above in

---

[6] Cf. also Kretschmer's etymology of Poseidon = πόσις Δᾶς "Spouse of Earth," *Glotta* 9 (1917) p. 217; M. Ventris and J. Chadwick, *Documents in Mycenaean Greek*[2] (Cambridge, 1972), p. 309.

[7] The name Alexandros is itself a problem: see H. Frisk, *Griechisches Etymologisches Wörterbuch*, s.v. ἀλέξω; P. Chantraine, *Dictionnaire Étymologique de la Langue Grecque* (Paris: Klincksieck, 1968), s.v. ἀνήρ.

[8] Helen uses it of herself (Γ 180, δ 145), Hephaistos of Aphrodite (θ 319), Agamemnon of Klytaimnestra (λ 424), Hephaistos of Hera (Σ 396). Cf. Achilles' epithet for Agamemnon, κυνώπης (Α 159).

[9] Ζ 344, 356. Cf. pp. 17 ff.

Chapter I; what Helen and Hera—and the whole house of Atreus—have most clearly in common is their close association with Argos.[10] Now, the adjective most often applied to the word κύων is ἀργός, and the noun that ἀργός most often modifies is κύων. Within the dictional patterns of Homeric epic, then, the idea of dogs must be firmly linked with the word ἀργός—whatever its meaning in context. Thus a lady strongly identified with Argos might well come to have dog-words applied to her through natural associations in the epic diction. Furthermore, if one recalls how often Hera is βοῶπις and Athena γλαυκῶπις, one wonders whether κυνῶπις may be a similar kind of epithet for Helen. The fact that the word Argos and dogs may be connected makes the possibility quite appealing.

2

a. ῥιγεδανῆς

This word occurs only once in epic, and so perhaps cannot justifiably be called an epithet. It certainly fits Helen in the context of the *Iliad*, where she is the visual reminder of death and suffering.[11]

It is impossible to say whether this is an adjective drawn from the epic tradition of Helen or a specialized word for this moment in this epic.

b. στυγερή

This word occurs as an epithet for the lady only once, and once more the question arises whether the expression really is traditionally connected with Helen, or whether it is being used in its context for a particular purpose. The problem of στυγερή and ῥιγεδανῆς is discussed more fully in the context of the *Iliad*, above.[12]

3

The implications of Helen's epithet Διὸς κούρη are far-reaching, particularly regarding her relationship with her brothers, Kastor and Polydeukes. Although they are referred to as the sons of Tyndareos (λ 298 ff) and Helen in Homer is never daughter of anyone but Zeus, she herself nevertheless identifies them as her brothers (Γ 238). This confusion exists more explicitly in later Greek mythology, where Helen and the Dioskouroi are called interchangeably

---

[10] See pp. 55 ff.
[11] Cf. Ω 775, πάντες δέ με πεφρίκασιν, and pp. 16 ff.
[12] See pp. 19 ff.

children of Zeus or Tyndareos,[13] and no effort seems to be made to keep the fathers sorted out. One explanation to the problem may be that Tyndareos is simply a heroic hypostasis of Zeus, his name perhaps originally meaning "thunderer."[14] More certainly, it is commonplace for a hero to have more than one father (e.g., Theseus/ Aigeus/Poseidon and Herakles/Amphitryon/Zeus), and such inconsistencies in mythology never seem to have bothered the Greeks very much. At any rate, what is clear is that although the *Iliad* knows that Helen is the sister of Kastor and Polydeukes and although the *Odyssey* knows that Tyndareos is the father of the Twins and of Klytaimnestra (ω 199), nowhere in Homer is Helen called daughter of Tyndareos. The epic tradition knows Helen only as the daughter of Zeus, and the exact relationship between her and the rest of the family remains somewhat blurred.

Kastor and Polydeukes appear as shadowy figures in the Homeric epics. The *Iliad* mentions them only once, where Helen wonders why they are not at Troy, and the poet states:

... τοὺς δ' ἤδη κάτεχεν φυσίζοος αἶα
ἐν Λακεδαίμονι αὖθι, φίλῃ ἐν πατρίδι γαίῃ (Γ 243 f).

The poet of the *Iliad* needed to have them out of the picture for artistic reasons;[15] the *Odyssey* does not even raise the question of their relationship to Helen, but gives a more elaborate description of their situation:

καὶ Λήδην εἶδον, τὴν Τυνδαρέου παράκοιτιν,
ἥ ῥ' ὑπὸ Τυνδαρέῳ κρατερόφρονε γείνατο παῖδε,
Κάστορά θ' ἱππόδαμον καὶ πὺξ ἀγαθὸν Πολυδεύκεα,
τοὺς ἄμφω ζωοὺς κατέχει φυσίζοος αἶα·
οἳ καὶ νέρθεν γῆς τιμὴν πρὸς Ζηνὸς ἔχοντες
ἄλλοτε μὲν ζώουσ' ἑτερήμεροι, ἄλλοτε δ' αὖτε
τεθνᾶσιν· τιμὴν δὲ λελόγχασιν ἶσα θεοῖσι (λ 298-304).

The passage in the *Iliad* does not state explicitly whether the brothers are alive or dead, but neither does it contradict the testimony of the *Odyssey*. All it says is that the earth "holds them under," and

---

[13] E.g., Theocritus XVIII 5, 18, 19; *H.H.* XXXIII 1, 2, etc.
[14] J. Schmidt in W. H. Roscher, *Ausführliches Lexikon der griechischen und römischen Mythologie* (Berlin: Teubner, 1924-1937), 5. 1416; A. Furtwängler, Roscher 1. 1154. The argument of G. Maresch, "Der Name der Tyndariden," *Glotta* 14 (1925) 298-299 is unconvincing.
[15] See pp. 9 ff.

the *Odyssey* account agrees. In fact, the poetry of Alcman and Pindar suggests that exactly the same is the case in Therapnai, their cult-site, where the brothers live under the earth.[16] Homeric tradition obviously also knew about the alternating life and death of the Dioskouroi.

The fact that Helen's father is Zeus and that she is associated with brothers who are essentially immortal gives her a divine pedigree from the start. The association implies, moreover, that in some respects Helen is a lady far older than her character in traditional Greek epic. A quick consideration of this association should help establish not only Helen's age but perhaps her pre-Homeric epic nature, as well.

It has been shown that the Dioskouroi are in fact genetic counterparts to the Aśvins of Vedic mythology, and must therefore have their roots in common Indo-European mythology.[17] The Aśvins, or "horsemen," are divine twins who specialize in rescuing people in distress and who are particularly concerned with the rising and setting of the Sun. Their association with the Sun, Sūryă, is symbolized by the fact that they are accompanied by the Sun-princess, Sūryā. Mythologically, under the epithet Nắsatyā—"the retrievers" [18]—they are concerned with the *recovery* of the Sun in the form of Sūryā. This relation to the rising and setting of the Sun also motivated their naturalistic identification with the Morning and Evening Stars.[19]

The Dioskouroi fit into much the same pattern. As sons of Zeus they are basically linked with the sky, and therefore with both light and darkness. The Aśvins are said to be individually the son of Night and of Dawn,[20] and the same light-and-dark alternation is reflected in the Greek notion of the Twins' alternating life and death. Since the path of the Sun is also associated with light and dark, the theme of losing and recovering the Sun naturally becomes attached to the Twins' mythology.[21] The Evening Star dives after the Sun at dusk, while the Morning Star leads it back at dawn. Now, the connection

---

[16] Alcman 7P and Pindar *Nem.* X. 51 ff.
[17] H. Güntert, *Der arische Weltkönig und Heiland* (Halle a.S., 1924), pp. 260-276; A. Macdonell, *Vedic Mythology* (Strassburg: Trubner, 1897), 49-54. Both also compare a pair of Latvian Dioskouroi.
[18] D. Frame, p. 151.
[19] G. Nagy, "Phaethon, Sappho's Phaon, and the White Rock of Leukas," *HSCP* 77 (1973), pp. 172 f., n. 94; W. Mannhardt, *Zeitschrift für Ethnologie* 7 (1875), 309 ff.
[20] Macdonell, p. 49, citing *Nirukta* 12, 2.
[21] D. Frame, pp. 11-31, and G. Nagy, "Phaethon," pp. 172 f., n. 94.

between the Dioskouroi and Helios is attested in Lakonian cult,[22] and with sun and light in general in numerous mythological accounts,[23] so the attachment to the Sun itself is no problem. As the Twins lose and recover the Sun, however, it becomes a passive entity in the myth, leading, as in the Indic myth, to the personification of a female Sun-princess, Sūryā instead of a male Sūryă. In Vedic myth the Aśvins are sometimes the husbands of Sūryā, sometimes her groomsmen.[24] It is clear that if she is to be paralleled in Greek mythology, the only character who can possibly fit the loss-recovery motif with reference to the Dioskouroi is Helen.

There are two problems with the idea that Helen represents the Sun-princess in the Greek version of Dioskouric mythology. The first is that while she is certainly the object of the Twins' quest in the story of her rape by Theseus, still in the much better-attested saga of her rape by Paris the Dioskouroi take no part.[25] The second is that on the surface Helen appears to display no characteristic of a Sun-princess at all. Homer gives no evidence specifically to the point, but he does offer some help in the solution of these problems.

Stig Wikander has shown that the heroic offspring of the gods in the Mahābhārata, specifically the sons of the Aśvins, Nakula and Sahadeva, are actually just anthropomorphizations of aspects of their divine parents,[26] and that in fact these anthropomorphizations refer to a mythological stage anterior to the religion of the Vedic hymns.[27] Now, although Helen does not have her brothers Kastor and Polydeukes to save her in Homer, she does have her husband Menelaos and his brother Agamemnon. Is it possible that the Atreidai may be Homeric hypostases of the Dioskouroi?

It might be argued that while the Dioskouroi are clearly twins and closely identified with one another, Agamemnon and Menelaos function as two separate entities.[28] Wikander has shown [29] that in

---

[22] S. Wide, *Lakonische Kulte* (Leipzig, 1893), p. 319.
[23] E.g., Pindar, *Nem.* X. 49; they steal the Leukippidai Φοίβη and Ἰλάειρα to be their brides, Paus. III 161; cf. Bethe in Pauly-Wissowa s.v. Dioskuren 1090-1091.
[24] Macdonell, p. 51, citing IV 43⁶, VII 69, I 34⁵, etc.
[25] Pauly-Wissowa s.v. Dioskuren, 1112 ff.
[26] Wikander, "Légende," pp. 37-53; "Nakula et Sahadeva," *Orientalia Suecana* 6 (1957) 66-96.
[27] Wikander, "Légende," p. 48.
[28] The Atreidai are sometimes twins; cf. the tradition passed on by Vergil, *Aeneid* VI 415.
[29] "Nakula," pp. 69-72.

many respects Nakula and Sahadeva function in complementary distribution to one another; whereas in Vedic myth the Aśvins are characterized as generally the same but "Dioskouric" in polarities such as life and death or dark and light, at the epic level the twin heroes are Dioskouric in many more respects. Moreover, when they do function together, their diction and themes tend to be identical, but when they are apart the epithets and themes may be more specialized (for example, together Nakula and Sahadeva both have warrior epithets, but Sahadeva alone never does; Sahadeva is wise and brilliant, but Nakula seldom is; Nakula alone always is the most beautiful, but together both brothers are; Draupadi is the wife of both, but only Nakula rescues her). In short, a basic Dioskouric paradox is that the twins are alike and differentiated at once.

Now, certain sophistications in Homeric epic have made it impractical to identify the Atreidai too strongly with one another. For example, the Homeric attitude toward kingship cannot tolerate two kings ruling simultaneously over the same host, and so Agamemnon must be the sole leader. Nevertheless, when the two Atreidai function together they are both referred to as co-leaders in the campaign. When Chryses comes to them as a suppliant, they are even named in the dual:

'Ατρείδα δὲ μάλιστα δύω, κοσμήτορε λαῶν (Α 16 = 375).

Nevertheless, although both Agamemnon and Menelaos are called Atreides, and although together they are the Atreidai, the epithet seems to tend to belong primarily to Agamemnon.[30] Even more obvious are the differences in epithet: Agamemnon is ἄναξ frequently, Menelaos never; Menelaos is ξανθός, Agamemnon never.[31]

---

[30] In the *Iliad*, Agamemnon is named 156 times, called "Atreides" 117 times; Menelaos is named 134 times' called "Atreides" 28. In the *Odyssey*, Agamemnon is named 20 times, called "Atreides" 20; Menelaos is named 60, called "Atreides" 20.

[31] This word may itself be a clue to Menelaos' Dioskouric status. In the masculine in epic it applies only to Menelaos, horses, rivers, and Rhadamanthys. The Aśvins are called "red," "having a red path," and "having a gold path" (Macdonell, p. 49), the last of which applies elsewhere only to rivers. The Dioskouroi as well as the Aśvins are horsemen, and the relationship between horses and running water is problematical but certainly real (see F. Schachermeyr, *Poseidon und die Entstehung des griechischen Götterglaubens*, Bern: A. Francke, 1950). Furthermore, ξανθός would seem to be an epithet appropriate to a celestial figure. Both times Rhadamanthys is mentioned in Homer (δ 564, η 323), he is described as ξανθός, and it is curious that the only two Homeric figures who are explicitly associated with 'Ηλύσιον—Menelaos and Rhadamanthys (δ 564)—are both ξανθός.

Similarly, Homer would not allow Helen to be married to both brothers, and so she must be married to one and somehow command loyalty from the other. Out of this complication may have arisen the oath of Helen's suitors,[32] and the confusion is further treated in the story that both Agamemnon and Menelaos wooed her, or that Agamemnon wooed her *for* Menelaos.[33] Indeed, the difference between Helen's sisterhood to the Dioskouroi and marriage to Menelaos is not so great, after all. The two Pāṇḍavas Nakula and Sahadeva were married to their lady, but only one rescued her;[34] both Agamemnon and Menelaos rescue Helen, but only one is married to her. In fact, the question of sisterhood or marriage is not a central one, as Wikander states in his discussion of the Pāṇḍavas:

> Comme on l'a remarqué depuis longtemps, la relation des dioscures indo-européens avec une déese est un trait typique de leur mythologie. Mais quand cette relation mythique se transpose, dans les légendes, sur le plan humain, elle s'exprime de diverses manières: la déesse peut être comprise comme la soeur des dieux jumeaux, ou leur femme, ou celle qui les séduit, etc.[35]

Nevertheless, although the Atreidai have a relationship with Helen parallel to that of the Dioskouroi, and although their major mythical exploit—retrieving Helen—fits into the Dioskouric pattern, solid Homeric evidence for the identification is admittedly slight. One final suggestion may come from the *Odyssey*: whereas Agamemnon died a most horrible death, Menelaos will live forever (δ 561-569), a sophistication of the day-by-day alternation which the Dioskouroi enjoy.[36]

There remains one single shred of evidence from Stesichoros, as read by Eustathios (*Il.* 1323. 55):

> τὸν δὲ εἰρημένον Ἐπειὸν ὑδροφορεῖν τοῖς Ἀτρείδαις ἱστορεῖ Στησίχορος, ἐν τῶι· "ᾤκτειρε δ' αὐτὸν ὕδωρ ἀεὶ φορέοντα Διὸς κούροις βασιλεῦσιν." ἔνθα ὅρα τὸ Διὸς κούροις, καθ' ὃ καὶ Διὸς κούρη ἡ

---

[32] Hesiod, fr. 204. 78 ff. M/W.
[33] Hesiod, fr. 197. 4 f M/W.
[34] Wikander, "Nakula," p. 74.
[35] Wikander, "Légende," p. 51. Cf. Butterworth, p. 4.
[36] The presence of Klytaimnestra as wife of Agamemnon is a problem in this entire argument. It is intuitively appealing to consider her a hypostasis of Helen, but there is little or no evidence to support the idea. Perhaps the fact that both Helen and Klytaimnestra are the mother of Iphigeneia (Paus. II 22. 7) points to an original identification of the two. Cf. Butterworth, p. 4.

'Αφροδίτη ἐν παραθέσει, ὥστε κατ' ἐξοχήν τινα Διόσκουροι συνθέτως οἱ τῆς Λήδας καὶ τοῦ Διός.[37]

Some kind of confusion between the Atreidai and the divine Dioskouroi is evident, but the source is not as authoritative as it might be, and it is all that is extant. Perhaps the case for Helen as a Sun-princess may be strengthened by thematic evidence surrounding her in Homer.

Helen's epithet Διὸς θυγάτηρ seems to "belong" to Aphrodite and Athena more than to anyone else. Now, it has been demonstrated [38] that the epithet Διὸς θυγάτηρ is the exact cognate of Vedic *divá(s) duhitár-*, which is restricted to Uṣas, the Dawn-goddess, alone. Uṣas is generally a beneficent goddess, but in her character of *divá(s) duhitár-* she is ambivalent. Her character has implications for the present study. Nagy has explained it thus:

> There is a parallel ambivalence in the cognate epithet Διὸς θυγάτηρ. In one instance, it can describe a beneficent Athena who has just rescued Menelaos and who is compared to a mother fostering her child (Δ 128). This function of the Διὸς θυγάτηρ as patroness of the Hero is typical. In another instance, however, the epithet describes a maleficent Persephone, goddess of the dead (λ 217). In still another instance, it describes Artemis when Penelope wants to be shot and killed by her (υ 61). Although the epithet Διὸς θυγάτηρ does not survive in combination with Eos, the goddess herself is likewise ambivalent. Homeric diction features her snatching up youths as if she were some Harpy, and yet she gives them immortality.[39]

Aside from the fact that this epithet connects Helen with the Dawn goddess, it also acts as a signal to the quality of Helen's behavior in the scene where the epithet occurs. She is called Διὸς θυγάτηρ at the moment when she is mixing the potion νηπενθές for Telemachos, Peisistratos, and Menelaos (δ 227). In the lines that follow, Helen appears clearly to be both a beneficent and malevolent lady, first helping Odysseus spy on the Trojans, later trying to betray the presence of the Argives in the Horse.

---

[37] Page, fr. 200 reads, with Athenaeus X 456 Ff, Διὸς κούρα.
[38] G. Nagy, "Phaethon," pp. 165 f; R. Schmitt, *Dichtung und Dichtersprache in indogermanischer Zeit*, pp. 169-173.
[39] See Nagy, "Phaethon," p. 166 for references and argumentation.

If the epithet applies so well to Helen, does it necessarily mean that she is a relative of the Dawn-goddess? Aphrodite holds the epithet more often than anyone, and it is now known that at least with respect to poetic diction she has taken over the realm of Greek Eos and is the equivalent of Vedic Uṣas.[40] From thematic study of the *Iliad* and the *Odyssey* it should already be clear how closely Helen is bound to Aphrodite. If it were not for the fact that Athena holds the epithet almost as often as Aphrodite does, it might be said that Helen must be another Greek version of the Dawn-goddess. Nevertheless, consideration of the contexts where Athena is called Διὸς θυγάτηρ reveals that whenever she is called by that epithet she is actively aiding a mortal.[41] Thus the effect of this epithet on Helen is twofold: on the one hand, it may link her with Aphrodite and thus with the Dawn-goddess; on the other, it simply designates her as a Διὸς θυγάτηρ figure, who is characterized by both helping and menacing mankind.

The other epithets which Helen shares primarily with Athena are κούρη Διός and Διὸς ἐκγεγαυῖα. It is immediately obvious that the one element all these epithets have in common is a statement of parentage. It is generally agreed that the great daughters of Zeus — Artemis, Athena, Aphrodite — are all powerful goddesses from a place or period when Zeus was not king, and that when the Indo-European sky-god came into conflict with them he made them his daughters, for they were too powerful to become mere consorts. Furthermore, in Homer the only ladies who are called Διὸς κούρη in the singular are Helen, Athena, Artemis, and Aphrodite. Helen is the only so-called "mortal" among them, and in an Indo-European context it stands to reason that if Zeus is going to take the trouble to beget a mortal, he will get a son. Thus Helen is unique in Homer, being a lady of divine parentage whose genealogy is rarely discussed, and of all the figures on the heroic plane who are children of Zeus, the only female. From the standpoint of diction, she has a great deal more in common with the great goddess-daughters of Zeus than with her heroic counterparts.[42]

The epithet Διὸς ἐκγεγαυῖα Helen shares with Athena alone. The

---

[40] D. Boedeker, *Aphrodite's Entry into Greek Epic* (Leiden: Brill, 1974), pp. 31-35.

[41] The Achaians (H 24, Δ 515), Diomedes (E 818), nurturing Erekhtheus (B 548), Telemachos (γ 337, 378), Odysseus (ν 359, χ 205, ω 502).

[42] Parry, *The Making of Homeric Verse*, p. 97, mentions that she is the only woman in Homer with her own set of epithets.

epic tradition is insisting on Helen's divine parentage, specifically with reference to Athena, who appears to be most emphatically "daughter of Zeus" (although it may be argued that Athena appears more often in epic than any other single lady, and thus will be more emphatically anything). The special connotations which Διὸς κούρη have for Helen, however, have yet to be supported adequately. The epithet Διὸς θυγάτηρ has raised the possibility of a link with the Dawn-goddess, but it is also clear that the tradition may simply be emphasizing Helen's unmarked divinity. Is there any other evidence for seeing Helen as the Dioskouric Sun-princess?

One possibility is Helen's final epithet, 'Αργείη. She shares it with Hera, but the latter is Argive only in one repeated expression:

"Ηρη τ' 'Αργείη καὶ 'Αλαλκομενηὶς 'Αθήνη (Δ 8 = Ε 908).

For the names of Athena and Hera together in the nominative, this is the only formula in epic which fills an entire line. The use of 'Αργείη for Helen is more fluid, being surrounded by many more than one expression.

Farnell mentions Alalkomenai in Boeotia as one of the oldest cult centers for worship of Athena, its name derived from her cult title and the form in Homer in turn derived from the name of the town.[43] Since Athena's title is cultic, then it is probable that 'Αργείη for Hera has the same force: "Hera-as-worshipped-in-Argos." The use of 'Αργείη for Helen, on the other hand, touches on the whole problem of where Homeric Argos is, or *if* it is.[44] Homer has Helen and Menelaos living in Lakedaimon (δ 1), specifically in Sparta (α 285). No mention is made in the epic of why Helen should be called 'Αργείη when she does not live in Argos. Perhaps the Argos here referred to may be the larger Argos—the whole region of the Argive Plain, or if that will not work, the entire Peloponnese, or all of Greece. It has been suggested [45] that Helen is called 'Αργείη where Homer wishes to stress her Argive sympathies. The contexts for the epithet, however, fail to support this idea—although there are several occurrences where she is linked with the Argives (e.g. Β 155-163), it is also clear that one of her major functions in the *Iliad* (where nine out of the eleven mentions occur) is to be the Cause of

---

[43] L. R. Farnell, *Cults of the Greek States* (Oxford, 1896-1909), I 308.
[44] D. Page, *History and the Homeric Iliad* (Berkeley: U. Cal. Press, 1959), pp. 127 ff, discusses the geographical aspects of the question.
[45] Whallon, "Homeric Epithets," p. 114.

War, the prize for which Argives and Trojans are fighting. A connection with the Argives and the Greek cause is too logical to support an argument about diction.

One explanation for 'Ἀργείη as it applies to Helen may be that the epithet does not refer to a city at all. The adjectival derivative of the root involved, ἀργός (< *ἀργρός), means "bright", an appropriate adjective for any divine figure, and particularly for one associated with the Dioskouroi; the noun derivative, Ἄργος, is etymologically an abstract formation on the same root, of the type γένος.[46] Whatever its meaning, the Homeric Ἄργος specializes in nourishing horses, an activity that would be favored by the Horsemen of myth (e.g. Γ 75); it is a place that has a μυχός, a word that elsewhere is used only of obviously enclosed spaces, like a tent (e.g. I 663), or a cave (e.g. ε 226); most importantly, Ἄργος is the place from which the Ἀργεῖοι, the heroes at Troy, have come, the place to which they long to return (e.g. B 287), and the land far from which many of them die (e.g. I 246).

In his ingenious treatment of the Greek root *nes-, Douglas Frame shows that the meaning of νόστος should be "return to life and light."[47] The great νόστος of Odysseus is a journey through the land of the dead and an emergence on the other side, into the light. If the place to which all heroes hope to return (νέεσθαι) is Argos, then Argos should be the place of life and light. The words actually occur together:

οὐδέ τοι ἐκτελέουσιν ὑπόσχεσιν ἥν περ ὑπέσταν
ἐνθάδ' ἔτι στείχοντες ἀπ' Ἄργεος ἱπποβότοιο,
Ἴλιον ἐκπέρσαντ' εὐτείχεον ἀπονέεσθαι (B 286-288).[48]

It is also clear that the idea of νόστος is closely allied with escaping death:

Ἀτρεΐδη, νῦν ἄμμε παλιμπλαγχθέντας ὀίω
ἂψ ἀπονοστήσειν, εἴ κεν θάνατόν γε φύγοιμεν (A 59-60).

As Priam sets off on his death-trip to Achilles' tent,[49] Hermes ap-

---

[46] H. Frisk, P. Chantraine, s.v. ἀργός and Ἄργος.
[47] D. Frame, *passim*.
[48] Also at B 112-115, I 19-22.
[49] Priam's friends mourn him as if he were going to his death (Ω 327 f); Hermes, guide to and from death, accompanies him (334 ff); Hermes approaches him at the tomb of Ilos (349); they cross a river (351); the trip takes place after dark, when all other men sleep (363). Cf. Whitman, p. 217.

pears to be his guide and assures him that he would accompany him all the way to Argos, either by ship or by foot:

σοὶ δ' ἂν ἐγὼ πομπὸς καί κε κλυτὸν "Αργος ἱκοίμην,
ἐνδυκέως ἐν νηΐ θοῇ ἢ πεζὸς ὁμαρτέων (Ω 437-8).

Clearly, there is no way to get from Troy to any geographical Argos on foot, but Hermes does accompany Priam to a metaphorical death and back to the light of day (Ω 677-697). In fact, Hermes leaves him just as the two cross the river Xanthos again, and the dawn breaks immediately upon Hermes' disappearance (Ω 692-695). So Argos appears, perhaps, to be the "bright place," the epic Land of the Living. Helen's epithet 'Αργείη (< * Αργεσ-ιη) may very well designate her as a "bright Helen," firmly associated with the land of life and light, and it also might substantiate the notion that she is one of the immortals.

Now, although the *Odyssey* states that Helen and Menelaos live in Sparta, the king himself says he is lord over a place called Argos (δ 174 ff). It seems likely, in light of the discussion of Argos above, that this realm of Menelaos has nothing to do with historical Argos at all, but rather is a purely legendary land, the place from which shining (δῖοι) heroes set out on heroic quests. Somewhere in this land of life and light is the palace of Menelaos, where everything shines, and which so overawed Telemachos that he wondered whether Zeus' palace might not be similar.[50] The palace shines in particular with some words that also apply to the sun. The walls are παμφανόωντα (δ 42), a word which otherwise modifies stars (X 26), chariots (Θ 320 = Ψ 509), fire (e.g. Σ 206), ἠλέκτωρ (e.g. Z 513), and the sun (ν 29). The palace is bright with ἠλέκτωρ (δ 73), specifically a sun-word, appearing also in collocation with ὑπερίων (T 398, H. Ap. 369) and even ἠέλιον (σ 296). It also shines with the gleam of bronze (χαλκοῦ στεροπή); στεροπή is regularly used with χαλκός, but only here does it apply to a palace rather than weapons, and it is also a special word for Zeus' thunderbolt (e.g. στεροπηγερέτα Ζεύς Π 298).[51] Aside from these specific expressions, there are many flashes of silver and gold throughout the palace, far too many to go unnoticed.

Helen herself shines, as well. The peplos she made "shines like a

---

[50] Cf. pp. 25 f.
[51] ἀστεροπή is always lightning.

star" (ο 108).⁵² At Γ 141 she wears an ἀργεννὴ ὀθόνη, which at Γ 419 is called a ἑανῷ ἀργῆτι φαεινῷ. From the morphological point of view, ἀργέννη is a direct Aeolic derivative of an abstract noun ἄργος (< *αργεσνᾱ) and ἀργής is clearly from the same *arg- root. The ὀθόνη occurs only at two other points in Homer: it is worn by the παρθένοι who dance in the chorus of Ariadne on the Shield of Achilles (Σ 595) and it is anointed with oil by the Phaiakian ladies (η 107). The Phaiakians are closer to the gods than other men, and the chorus is actually embossed in gold, so the brightness motif may here, too, point toward divinity. The fact that the maidens dance at the chorus of Adriadne is probably significant as well, for it would link them with a fertility festival, and Ariadne appears to be an old goddess of fertility.⁵³

The case of the ἑανός is somewhat more striking. When Aphrodite comes to summon Helen from the Wall to Paris' bedchamber, she gets her attention thus:

χειρὶ δὲ νεκταρέου ἑανοῦ ἐτίναξε λαβοῦσα (Γ 385).

Later, when Aphrodite has grown angry at Helen's resistance and threatens to turn away from her, Helen relents in fear and follows:

βῆ δὲ κατασχομένη ἑανῷ ἀργῆτι φαεινῷ
σιγῇ, πάσας δὲ Τρῳὰς λάθεν· ἦρξε δὲ δαίμων (Γ 419 f).

As Helen leaves the Wall, the ἑανός somehow renders her invisible to the Trojan women, even though it is emphatically bright and shining. Perhaps the ἑανός is seen from Helen's perspective. Perhaps Aphrodite's presence makes Helen invisible, for she has just whisked Paris from battle through similar means:

... τὸν δ' ἐξήρπαξ' Ἀφροδίτη
ῥεῖα μάλ' ὥς τε θεός, ἐκάλυψε δ' ἄρ' ἠέρι πολλῇ (Γ 380 f).

Yet in the scene with Helen there is no indication that Aphrodite has effected the invisibility, and certainly no mention of a cloud in which she hides the lady.

The noun ἑανός occurs only four times in the *Iliad*, never in the

---

⁵² The only other peplos which shines like a star is the one Hekabe offers Athena (Z 295). It was acquired by Paris in Sidonia when he was bringing Helen to Troy.

⁵³ M. Nilsson, *The Minoan-Mycenean Religion and its Survival in Greek Religion* (Lund: Gleerup, 1950), pp. 523-528. Cf. the discussion of Helen's associations with fertility, Chapter 4.

Odyssey.⁵⁴ Aside from the two passages where Helen wears it, it appears once worn by Hera,

ἀμφὶ δ' ἄρ' ἀμβρόσιον ἑανὸν ἕσαθ', ὅν οἱ 'Αθήνη
ἔξυσ' ἀσκήσασα, τίθει δ' ἐνὶ δαίδαλα πολλά (Ξ 178 f),

and once by Artemis,

ἀμφὶ δ' ἄρ' ἀμβρόσιος ἑανὸς τρέμε . . . (Φ 507).

It is obvious that it must be a ladies' garment, and that it is worn by some very distinguished ladies. Artemis' ἑανός shakes when, hurt and embarrassed by the whipping Hera has given her, she approaches Zeus for comfort; Hera's is doubly spectacular for belonging to one goddess and being the work of another. Both Hera's and Artemis' garments are ἀμβρόσιοι: is it mere chance that Helen's is νεκτάρεος, and occupies the same metrical position as ἀμβρόσιος, as well?

Outside of Homer, the word occurs in Linear B:⁵⁵

e-ra₃-wo u-po-jo po-ti-ni-ja
we-a₂-no-i a-ro-pa OIL = A 0/1/0 (PY Fr 1225)
"Oil, for the Lady of Upo, unguent for garments."⁵⁶

Here we-a₂-no-i are connected closely to a *potnia*, a goddess. In Homer the ἑανός is connected with Athena, Artemis, and Hera, as well as with one earthbound lady. It is ἀμβρόσιος and νεκτάρεος, and Helen's, although shining, may be capable of rendering its wearer invisible. It seems clear that the garment is intended for the use of a goddess. The ὀθόνη, Homer's other word for the same piece of clothing, enters the argument here, for the actions of the Phaiakian women are certainly reminiscent of the Linear B collocation of oil and garments.

Helen is characterized, then, as being clothed in shining, immortal

---

⁵⁴ The noun εἱανός appears once in Achilles' comparison of Patroklos to a girl hanging to her mother's skirts: εἱανοῦ ἀπτομένη (Π 9). The form need not concern us here, since it is of different spelling, different metrical value, and occurs only in the genre of the simile, while ἑανός appears only in direct narrative. The adjective ἑανός is from a different, undetermined root, and while the digamma of ἑανός makes position regularly, there is no such effect from ἑᾱνός (Chantraine, Frisk, s.v.).

⁵⁵ There is one other attestation, PY Un 1322, where it is modified [ri]-no re-po-to = *linon lepton*.

⁵⁶ I quote the translation of L. R. Palmer, *The Interpretation of Mycenean Greek Texts* (Oxford, 1963), p. 243.

garments. She also uses shining materials, and is even compared to a goddess with golden attributes, Ἀρτέμιδι χρυσηλακάτῳ, upon her first entrance in the *Odyssey* (δ 122). This is the only occurrence of Artemis with this epithet in the *Iliad* or *Odyssey*, but she is described thus elsewhere:

οὐδέ ποτ' Ἀρτέμιδα χρυσηλάκατον κελαδεινὴν
δάμναται ἐν φιλότητι φιλομμειδὴς Ἀφροδίτη (*H. Ven.* 16 f),

νῦν δέ μ' ἀνήρπαξε χρυσόρραπις Ἀργειφόντης
ἐκ χοροῦ Ἀρτέμιδος χρυσηλακάτου κελαδεινῆς (*H. Ven.* 117 f),

Ἄρτεμιν ἀείδω χρυσηλάκατον κελαδεινήν (*H.* xxvii. 1).

O. S. Due [57] has made a good case for the meaning of ἠλακάτη being the smooth part of a reed, suitable for use as an arrow shaft or distaff. Thus the epithet for Artemis can be read "she of the golden arrows" or "she of the golden distaff." Clearly, in most places Artemis is the huntress, and arrows are her attributes.

Study of the use of ἠλακάτη by itself in the *Iliad* and *Odyssey* shows that it invariably means "distaff," and that with one exception it always occurs in two formulaic patterns: it is either followed by a form of στρωφάω [58] or is bound to ἱστόν in the repeated line

ἱστόν τ' ἠλακάτην τε, καὶ ἀμφιπόλοισι κέλευε
(Z 491 = α 357 = φ 351).

The only exception to these two patterns is the Helen episode, where Helen's distaff appears twice, once as golden,

χρυσέην τ' ἠλακάτην ταλαρόν θ' ὑπόκυκλον (δ 131),

and once as covered with dark wool:

ἠλακάτη τετάνυστο ἰοδνεφὲς εἶρος ἔχουσα (δ 135).

The comparison of Helen to Artemis of the golden ἠλακάτη is only nine lines before Helen's servants bring her the golden distaff for her spinning. Homer certainly means to link the two ladies through their ἠλακάτη, and thus at δ 122 must consciously perceive the epithet as meaning "she of the golden distaff," even though it regularly refers to arrows.

---

[57] O. S. Due, "The Meaning of the Homeric Formula χρυσηλάκατος κελαδεινή," *Classica et Mediaevalia* 26 (1965) 1-9.
[58] ζ 53, 306; η 105; ρ 97; σ 315.

If Homer is changing the meaning of a metaphor for the sake of comparing Helen to Artemis, there must be a reason. One possibility may be that he is so conscious of Helen's attachment to gold that this theme naturally came to mind in a context where ἠλακάτη was already appropriate. It is also possible that he wants to link Helen with Artemis for other reasons. The ὀθόνη and ἑανός do so, as well, for Artemis wears a ἑανός and is a goddess quite similar to Ariadne of the Shield, the lady who has a chorus where maidens dance. She is also like Helen in that she, too, is a daughter of Zeus, and so if Homer wanted to compare Helen to any goddess, Artemis was a likely enough candidate. Furthermore, Artemis is not infrequently compared to a lady who is entering upon a scene. Odysseus tells Nausikaa that she looks especially like Artemis in εἶδος, μέγεθος, and φυή (ζ 151 f) and Penelope comes from her bedchamber looking like Artemis or golden Aphrodite (ρ 37 = τ 54). The theme seems to be a commonplace; Homer merely elaborates it in the case of Nausikaa, who is playing with young girls as Artemis is wont to do, and of Helen, who works with a golden distaff.

Helen also has shining attendants. At Γ 144 they are named Aithre, daughter of Pittheus, and Klymene; at δ 123 ff they are Adraste, Alkippe, and Phylo. Now, Pittheus should be king of Troizen and his daughter Aithre the consort of Poseidon and mother of Theseus. According to Plutarch [59] and Pausanias,[60] when the Dioskouroi rescued Helen from Theseus at Aphidna, they also captured his mother to be Helen's servant. In other words, when the Twins brought their sister back from the son of the Sea-god, they brought the "Burning Lady" with her.[61] Could the name of Helen's servant in the *Iliad* be a Homeric reference to the legend of her rape by Theseus? [62] It is possible that both the Theseus-legend and the Homeric language are retaining the memory of Helen's being associated with the Sun.

Similarly, Klymene should be the consort of the Sun [63] and mother

---

[59] *Theseus* 34.
[60] V 19. 4.
[61] Chantraine, s.v. αἴθω.
[62] W. Kullmann, *Die Quellen der Ilias* (*Hermes* Einzelschriften 14, 1960), pp. 74-79, especially 78 f; *pace* A. Dihle, *Homer-Probleme* (Opladen, 1970), pp. 29-34.
[63] Euripides, frg. 771 N.; H. J. Rose, *Handbook of Greek Mythology* (London: Methuen, 1953), p. 33.

of Phaethon or of Prometheus.⁶⁴ The masculine form Klymenos is another name for Hades, particularly at Hermione,⁶⁵ a town which is connected with the Helen-legend.⁶⁶ That the lady Klymene is a sun-goddess and the lord Klymenos is a god of the underworld should cause no problem by this point: the Sun spends half its time below the earth. Thus both of Helen's attendants in the *Iliad* suggest an attachment with the Sun.

Helen's attendants in the *Odyssey* are less obviously shining, but they are of some interest, nevertheless. Alkippe in Attica was a daughter of Ares who was violated by a son of Poseidon;⁶⁷ Adraste is reminiscent of Adrasteia, a title of Nemesis, who is sometimes Helen's mother, and also of Adrastos, who was a king of Argos and had a daughter named Argeia!⁶⁸ These two ladies may connect Helen with more of Greece than just Sparta, and Argeia is certainly suggestive of Helen's brightest epithet, Ἀργείη.

The evidence from Homeric diction, then, points to the possibility that Helen may be a goddess, and even gives some indication what sort of goddess she may be. Although Homer never states explicitly that she is the Sun-princess and Indo-European consort of the Dioskouroi, the themes in his inherited, traditional language clearly invest her with attributes which involve a brightness verging on solar imagery. Furthermore, Helen's epithet system links her with the great Homeric goddesses Athena, Artemis, Aphrodite, and Hera. The implications of these identifications are not entirely identical: Athena, Artemis, and Aphrodite are all daughters of Zeus, while Hera is clearly a wife or mother-figure. The varying directions in which Helen's diction seems to point may appear to be contradictory on the surface, but the accumulation of evidence is not yet complete. Before a clear judgment can be made on the nature of Helen, some considerations must be given to her character as a figure of cult and ritual.

---

⁶⁴ Prometheus: Hesiod, *Theogony* 351, 508. Phaethon: Hyginus, fab. 156, possibly already in Hesiod. See Latte in Pauly-Wissowa s.v. Klymene, col. 879.
⁶⁵ Pausanias II 35. 9.
⁶⁶ See below, p. 75, n. 97.
⁶⁷ Rose, *Handbook*, p. 158.
⁶⁸ Rose, *Handbook*, p. 190.

CHAPTER FOUR

HELEN'S DIVINE NATURE OUTSIDE OF HOMERIC POETRY

There is another body of evidence about Helen's nature which is not dependent upon her epic character, but rather appears to be native to Greece from preliterate times. The Helen-figure of cult and other religious contexts seems to be a lady quite different from the one found in Homer and later literature, and one is tempted with Farnell [1] to deny her an originally divine nature because that nature is difficult to define. Nevertheless, careful comparison of the native Greek evidence with the evidence already gleaned from epic will reveal that the apparent inconsistencies in fact exist only on the surface. Rather than conflicting with her epic character, Helen's cultic aspect will provide it with more depth. Her nature will appear no less complex, but at least many facets should begin to fall into a pattern.

Clues to the nature of the divine Helen may be implicit in her name, and so for a moment its etymology must be considered. It has proved a problem to scholars until the present. Curtius,[2] following numerous earlier writers [3] and a variety of artistic representations which helped document his theory, suggested ἑλ- from *swel-, and thus Ἑλένη cognate with σελήνη "moon". Helen's association with stars and moon in artistic contexts [4] and the attestations of ἑλένη/ἑλάνη "torch" [5] and Ἑλένη as a name for St. Elmo's Fire [6]

---

[1] Farnell, *Hero Cults*, p. 324.
[2] G. Curtius, *Grundzüge der griechischen Etymologie* (Leipzig: Teubner, 1879), s.v. Helena.
[3] Perhaps based on Neanthes the historian; see below, p. 65.
[4] See F. Chapouthier, *Les Dioscures au service d'une déesse* (Paris: Boccard, 1935), *passim*; also Lily B. Ghali-Kahil, *Les Enlèvements et le Retour d'Hélène dans les Textes et les Documents Figurés*, École Française d'Athènes, Travaux et Mémoires X (Paris, 1955).
[5] Hesychius, s.v.; Neanthes Historicus in Athenaeus, *Deipnosophistae* XV. 699 d.
[6] John the Lydian, *De Ostentiis* 5 B:
 ... τὸ δὲ τοιοῦτον σχῆμα ἤτοι κατάστημα οἱ τὴν θάλατταν πλέοντες Ἑλένην καλοῦσιν. ἀλλὰ κἀνταῦθα τὰ ἐξ αὐτῆς ἡ πρόνοια δείκνυσι· δύο γὰρ ἀστέρες

made the etymology a tempting one. Unfortunately, the phonological problems are severe, and the connection cannot stand. The progression from σέλας would be *selasnā > *selānā > σελήνη, whereas Helen's name is emphatically Ἑλένη: furthermore, Frisk [7] points out that the origin of the ς of σέλας and σελήνη is an unsolved problem, so that basing the etymology of Ἑλένη on this root is overly risky. Grégoire [8] suggested that the λ of Ἑλένη arose from an original ν and posited Ἐλένη (Ϝελένη) < * Ϝενένᾱ, and most closely related to Latin *Venus*. There is, however, no solid phonological precedent for such a pattern of dissimilation, and the morphology of* Ϝενένᾱ is unmotivated. Boisacq [9] considered Ἑλένη from ἑλένη "torch" and that word in turn from εἴλη "warmth of the sun." The diminutive form ἑλένιον he derives from ἕλος "marshland," an unlikely possibility for Helen because of the formation -ενη.[10] ἕλος is an *es*-stem noun of the third declension (type γένος), which means that in compounds its combinatory form would be ἐλεσ-. Thus * ἐλέσ-νη > * ἐλείνη,[11] or, with a suffix in -ενη, * ἐλεσ-ένη > * ἐλείνη. Furthermore, there is no parallel in Greek of an *es*-stem (type γένος) with derivatives in -ενη. A further problem with Boisacq's line of reasoning is that according to him two words which are formally equivalent, ἑλένη "torch" and ἑλένη "basket," remain etymological unrelated. J. Pokorny [12] follows him, attempting to derive Ἑλένη and ἑλένη "torch" from the Indo-European root *swel- "schwelen, brennen," and ἑλένη "basket" from the root *wel- "drehen, winden," even though the words are formally identical. Frisk [13] and Chantraine [14] both despair of an etymology.

Since none of these earlier suggestions offers much satisfaction, it would be best to begin with the evidence and try to build on it in a

---

εὐθὺς κατασκήπτουσι τῆς τοιαύτης φορᾶς, οὓς Κάστορα καὶ Πολυδεύκην καλοῦσιν, οἱ παραχρῆμα πρὸς φυγὴν τὴν λεγομένην (Ἑλένην) ἐλαύνουσι.

Cf. Pliny *NH* 2. 101: the single flame of St. Elmo's Fire is menacing, while the double flame is favorable.

[7] S.v. σέλας, σελήνη.

[8] *Bulletin de la Classe des lettres de l'Académie royale des sciences des lettres, et des beaux-arts de Belgique* 5 sér. 32 (1946) 255 ff.

[9] S.v. Ἑλένη, p. 237.

[10] P. 241.

[11] Cf. * φα-εσ-νός → φαεινός.

[12] *Indogermanisches etymologisches Wörterbuch* (Bern, 1959), pp. 1045 and 1140-1141.

[13] S.v. Ἑλένη.

[14] S.v. Ἑλένη.

new way. With derivatives of ἕλος and σελήνη ruled out, there remains a list of words formally related to Ἑλένη which, it will emerge, can lead to an understanding of Helen in her Spartan context as goddess. These words are as follows:

ἑλένη· λαμπάς, δέτη. Hesychius s.v.

ἑλένη· ἔστι δὲ καὶ ἑλένη πλεκτὸν ἀγγεῖον σπάρτινον, τὰ χείλη οἰσύινον, ἐν ᾧ φέρουσιν ἱερὰ ἄρρητα τοῖς Ἑλενηφορίοις. Pollux 10. 191.

ἑλάνη· ἄλλος δὲ ἑλάνην, ὁ δέ τις ἑλάνας, τὰς λαμπάδας οὕτω φάσκων καλεῖσθαι παρὰ τὴν ἕλην. Neanthes Historicus.[15]

ἑλάνη δὲ ἡ λαμπὰς καλεῖται, ὡς Ἀμερίας φησίν, Νίκανδρος δ' ὁ Κολοφώνιος ἑλάνην τὴν τῶν καλάμων δέσμην. Athenaeus 701 A.

Ἑλενηφόρια· Pollux 10. 191 (above).

ἑλένιον, ἑλένειον· a plant, variously described. Hesychius s.v., Et. Mag. 328. 16, etc.

ἑλένιος· ἀγγεῖον, χωροῦν τέταρτον. Hesychius s.v.

Ἑλένεια· ἑορτὴ ἀγομένη ὑπὸ τῶν Λακώνων. Hesychius s.v.

Of the seven words, three are adjectival in form. ἑλένιος appears to be an adjectival formation on ἑλένη "basket" of the type ἡμέρα: ἡμέριος. It must indicate a kind of container similar in size, shape, or appearance to a ἑλένη. Ἑλένεια is also clearly an adjectival formation on Ἑλένη of the type (Ἥρη) Καλλίστη: Καλλιστεῖα, or Κόρη: Κόρεια,[16] and the meaning would be basically "those things having to do with Helen." The plant ἑλένιον is something of a mystery. It is variously described as the flower in Alexandria [17] or on the island Helene [18] which grew from Helen's tears, or a plant which Helen sowed before snakes "ὅπως βοσκόμενοι ἀναιρεθῶσιν." [19] Theophrastus [20] specifies that it is woody, and has small leaves and a sweet

---

[15] In Athenaeus, *Deipnosophistae* XV. 699 d.
[16] Καλλιστεῖα: Schol. H 118; Nilsson, *Griechische Feste von religiöser Bedeutung* (Leipzig: Teubner, 1906), p. 57. Κόρεια: Plutarch *Dio* 56, Hesychius s.v.
[17] *Et. Mag.* 328. 16.
[18] Pliny *NH* 21. 33.
[19] Hesychius s.v.
[20] *Historia Plantarum* 6. 1. 1, 6. 1. 2.

scent. Dioskorides [21] adds that one of its roots drunk with wine will "help" against the bites of wild animals. From the point of view of morphology, this word also is an adjectival formation on a base ἐλεν-. It is formally impossible for ἐλένιον to have preceded ἑλένη, and in all likelihood both words are derivations from the same base. Mythological connections between Helen and the flower are by now elaborate if not thoroughly confused, and it is impossible to determine whether originally there was any relationship between the two entities. Nevertheless, it is certain that morphologically the proper name of the lady could not have evolved from the name of the plant.

There remain, then, a festival, Ἑλενηφόρια, a basket of rope and reeds, ἑλένη, and two spellings of a torch, ἑλένη and ἑλάνη. Each of them represents a use of the form ἑλένη which may be the basis of Helen's name.

The Ἑλενηφόρια presents a special problem. LSJ (9th ed., 1968) gloss it as a festival of Brauronian Artemis, although Pollux, the only source for the word, says nothing about Brauron or Artemis. Paul Stengel's article in Pauly-Wissowa has it as Athenian, again on no apparent evidence.[22] The origin of the confusion lies in an emendation of Athenaeus 6. 223 A by J. Casaubon. The passage quotes a fragment of a comedy by Diphilus, the remaining lines of which include a reference to Brauron and Artemis. The manuscript reading of the play's title was ΕΛΑΙΩΝΗΦΡΟΥΡΟΥΣΙ, which Casaubon emended to ΕΛΕΝΗΦΟΡΟΥΣΙΝ; the emendation was accepted as correct for Meineke's 1840 edition of the comic poets, and the reading was perpetuated in such basic source books as Passow's Greek lexicon,[23] Roscher (1950. 52 ff),[24] and the Stephanus Thesaurus.[25] T. Kock, in his later edition of the comic fragments,[26] removed the misreading and defended the manuscript reading with parallel titles from other plays:

---

[21] *De Materia Medica* 1. 29.

[22] Although he does cite the new reading explained below, he does not enter it into his primary definition. He also spells it Helenophoria, having followed the reading in the index to I. Bekker's 1846 edition of Pollux rather than the text, where it is spelled Helenephoria. P. Stengel, Pauly-Wissowa s.v. Ἑλενοφόρια, vol. 7, 2844.

[23] F. Passow, *Handwörterbuch der griechischen Sprache*⁵ (Leipzig, 1841), II. 870 s.v. Ἑλενηφόρια.

[24] Roscher, *Ausführliches Lexikon der griechischen und römischen Mythologie*.

[25] III. 713 s.v. Ἑλενηφόρια.

[26] Kock, *Comicorum Atticorum Fragmenta* (Leipzig: Teubner, 1888).

Φρουροῦντες, ut Νεμόμενοι Philemonis, Σχολάζοντες Calliae apud Suidam, Χορεύουσι Posidippi . . .
praeterea cum Diphili titulo cf. Ἰπνὸς ἢ Παννυχίς Pherecratis, Μυλών Antiphanis, Φρέαρ Diphili et Anaxippi . . .[27]

The matter, however, was complicated further by Suchier; A. Mommsen explains, trying to disentangle the problem as follows:

> Suchier *De Diana Brauronia* p. 38 betrachtete Ἑλενηφόρια (Pollux 10. 191) als Namen der brauronischen Kanephorenbrauche, weil die Anrede an die Göttin von Brauron ihm zufolge in Diphilos' Helenophorusen vorgekommen ist, Athen. 6. 1. 223 A. Aber Suchiers Helenophorusen beruhen auf einer gewagten Änderung von Ἑλενηφοροῦσιν, wie man einst las, in Ἑλενηφορούσαις. Und jetzt wird bei Athen. Δίφιλος δ' ἐν Ἐλαιωνηφρουροῦσι gelesen.[28]

Suchier had hit on a striking similarity between the Ἑλενηφόρια of Pollux and the rite called Kanephoria, but unfortunately a direct connection between the two is nowhere explicit,[29] so that his emendation is groundless. This similarity will be considered again below in the treatment of Helen's cult. The particular situation of the word Ἑλενηφόρια, however, should now be clear: it is attested only in the passage of Pollux quoted above,[30] only as the context in which baskets containing ἱερὰ ἄρρητα are carried, with no mention of who carries them, where, or when.

There now remain a basket of woven rope and wicker and two spellings of a torch. ἑλάνη is specifically a torch or bundle of reeds, and may be simply an inherited formal variant of ἑλένη; ἑλαν- may be a prevocalic zero-grade of the base ἑλεν-.[31] Hesychius' ἑλένη is glossed as δέτη "torch," or more technically, something bound together, and thus is most likely also a torch of reeds. The two basic meanings of ἑλένη then, are "torch of reeds" and "basket of rope and

---

[27] Kock, Diphilos 30.
[28] *Feste der Stadt Athen in Altertum* (Leipzig: Teubner, 1898), p. 458, n. 2.
[29] Mommsen, p. 123, n. 4.
[30] P. 65.
[31] Neanthes' etymology ἑλάνη ← ἕλη "stalk of pulse" is probably not correct, for a long ᾱ would be represented by η, or else the word would be spelled ἑλάνα, with non-Attic vocalism throughout. Thus the α of ἑλάνη appears to be short. The word is equivalent to ἑλένη as derived from the zero-grade of the root ἑλεν-. The reflex of vocalic ν in * ἑλν- would be αν before another vowel, resulting in ἑλάνη.

wicker." The common denominator in the two meanings must be the "wicker, reed," from which both are made. Use of the material as name for the manufactured article is not uncommon,[32] and so one can deduce the essential meaning of ἑλένη as "reed" or "shoot" of some kind.

Since both types of ἑλένη now can be derived from the root * wel-, Pokorny's placement of Helen "Lichtgottin" under the root * swel- may be rejected.[33] It seems unlikely that the lady alone would be derived from a root meaning "shine," while all other formally similar words imply growing, twisting up. But how can the name of a Lakonian goddess and heroine have anything to do with reeds and wicker baskets? A consideration of what is known of Helen's cult may suggest some answers to this question.

The evidence, scattered among a wide range of ancient writers, offers little firm ground on which to base an interpretation. Hesychius[34] reports that maidens were carried "εἰς τὸ Ἑλένης" in κάνναθρα, wicker carriages, some of which were decorated with "εἴδωλα ἐλάφων ἢ γυπῶν." He does not mention where the temple is, but a connection with the Ἑλένεια,[35] and thus with the Lakonians, is likely. The word κάνναθρα appears in three further contexts, as well: Plutarch[36] says they are decorated with "εἴδωλα γρυπῶν . . . καὶ τραγελάφων," and that young girls ride in them in processions. Xenophon[37] adds that they are going to Amyklai, and Athenaeus[38] remarks that they are used thus in the Spartan festival Hyakinthia. Whether there may be a basic identity of cult involved in all these attestations is difficult to determine, and the question will be considered further below.[39]

The only other seemingly related practice is the Helenephoria described by Pollux, above,[40] where baskets called ἑλέναι were carried. There is no direct evidence that this festival had any connection with Helen at all, since its name may mean simply, "the

---

[32] E.g., πεύκη "pine, torch made of pinewood;" λίνον "the plant flax, anything made of flax."
[33] J. Pokorny, p. 1045.
[34] S.v. κάνναθρα.
[35] Cf. p. 99.
[36] Agesilaus 19.
[37] Agesilaus 8. 7.
[38] Deipnosophistae IV. 138 e-139 b.
[39] Pp. 76-78.
[40] P. 65.

carrying of baskets." The implications of the vagueness of this term will be considered at length below.[41]

More material evidence for the reality of Helen-worship is the existence of a temple at Therapnai, in the neighborhood of Sparta. Excavations and study conducted there by the British School at Athens revealed that the site is as old as Late Mycenaean, and that the area immediately surrounding the temple was occupied not *later* than Late Mycenaean times. The temple itself flourished through Geometric and Lakonian periods.[42] Although in literature the site is almost invariably referred to as the Menelaion,[43] it seems likely that this was the temple to which Hesychius made reference, and that it was originally dedicated to Helen herself. Mycenaean remains from the Menelaion include a phi-shaped female figurine of terra-cotta [44] and finds from a later date include many examples of a female rider on horseback.[45] The similarity between these relics and those discovered at the temple of Artemis Orthia in Sparta would suggest similarity between the divinities worshiped or the acts performed there. The relationship between Helen and Artemis will be elaborated below.[46]

There is further connection of Helen with Sparta proper [47] and evidence of some cult in Rhodes, Kenchreai, Chios, and elswhere,[48] but nowhere does she seem to be as important as she is in the area around Sparta. Almost all the references to her place her at Therapnai, and it seems safe to suppose that she was essentially a local deity from that neighborhood. Myth carries her far across the Medi-

---

[41] Pp. 79-80.
[42] R. M. Dawkins, *Annual of the British School at Athens* 16 (1909/10) 5.
[43] Pausanias III. 19. 9 has Helen and Menelaos buried there, with a temple; Isocrates *Helen* 63 says sacrifices are made to Helen and Menelaos there "οὐχ ὡς ἥρωσιν ἀλλ' ὡς θεοῖς ἀμφοτέροις οὖσιν"; Herodotus VI. 61 mentions a ἱρόν to Helen there; Polybius V. 18. 10 names a Menelaion and Livy XXXIV. 28 a Mt. Menelaus, neither of them making further comment. The Schol. Eur. *Troades* 210 calls Therapnai "ἡ πόλις τῆς Ἑλένης," and the late epic writer Tryphiodorus 520 calls Helen "Θεραπναίη νύμφη."
[44] M. S. Thompson, *BSA* 15 (1908/9) 116 f.
[45] Thompson, p. 124. Geometric, much more numerous in later Lakonian.
[46] Pp. 74-77.
[47] Paus. III. 15. 3 says she had a ἱερόν there; Theocritus XVIII has Spartan maidens singing of her.
[48] Rhodes: Paus. III. 19. 10; Kenchreai: Helen's λουτρόν, Paus. II. 2. 3; Chios: a spring called Helene, Steph. Byz. 265. 5; Egypt: probably founded during Lakonian and Arkadian colonization, Plut. *De Herod. Malig.* 12, Steph. Byz. s.v., cf. S. Wide, p. 345; Attica: a "trittuia" sacrifice with the Dioskouroi, Eustath. ad Hom. 1425. 61 f; Ilion: Athenag. *Leg.* 1.

terranean, but even so her homeland is always the Peleponnese. More specifically, aside from a Homeric problem involving Argos,[49] she is always situated at Lakedaimon or Sparta.

If indeed Helen is a local goddess of Therapnai, her powers should be largely concerned with fertility and the general well-being of her people at home. So much one can merely guess, but some specific aspects to her divinity can be inferred from traditions found in literature. The evidence is of basically two varieties: stories bearing directly on Helen's nature or powers, and striking similarities or proximities between her and other divine figures. The information is scanty, but the method of interpretation, if used cautiously, seems secure enough to allow a qualified conclusion to be drawn about what kind of lady Helen is, and ultimately about whether the posited etymology of her name fits this character.

The eighteenth Idyll of Theocritus is an epithalamion addressed to Helen and Menelaos. The chorus of maidens singing to the bride and groom end their song with a description of how they will decorate a plane tree with a wreath of lotus, pouring oil at its foot, and inscribing on its bark "σέβευ μ'· Ἑλένας φυτόν εἰμι." [50] Curiously, the same Idyll refers to Helen both as Τυνδαρίδα (line 5) and as Ζανὸς ... θυγάτηρ (line 19), so it would seem likely that Theocritus is well aware that he is dealing with a figure of both myth and cult. Wilhelm Mannhardt [51] and later Georg Kaibel [52] interpreted this Idyll as an αἴτιον referring to a cult already existing in Lakonia; from internal evidence Kaibel identified the precise location as Sparta, near the Dromos and Platanistas.[53] Another story, reported by Pausanias,[54] tells how while she was visiting Rhodes Helen went bathing and was captured by the handmaidens of a vengeful Polyxo and hanged from a tree, thus explaining Helen's worship there under the title of δενδρῖτις. Parallel motifs in the stories of Ariadne and her sister Phaidra, both of whom are hanged in one account or another, encourage the view that a hanging myth implies tree cult.[55] Further-

---

[49] See pp. 55-57.
[50] Theoc. XVIII. 48.
[51] Wilhelm Mannhardt, *Wald- und Feldkulte* (Berlin: Borntraeger, 1905), pp. 22 ff.
[52] Georg Kaibel, "Theokrits ΕΛΕΝΗΣ ΕΠΙΘΑΛΑΜΙΟΝ," *Hermes* 27 (1892) 249-259.
[53] Paus. III. 15. 3; Kaibel, p. 255.
[54] III. 19. 9.
[55] Paus. I. 22. 2, II. 32. 3; S. Wide, p. 343; M. Nilsson, *Geschichte der griechischen Religion* (Munich: Beck, 1967), pp. 314 f, 487.

more, Pausanias mentions a plane-tree and spring called Μενελαΐς in Kaphyai, not far from Kondylea, where there was a grove and sanctuary of Artemis ἀπαγχομένη.[56] Coupled with this fact is the record of springs named for Helen in Kenchreai (Ἑλένης λουτρόν) and Chios (a spring where Helen washed herself).[57] All this evidence points in the same direction: Helen is closely connected with fertility, with the power of growth. One recalls that part of the yearly ritual for some fertility goddesses was a renewing of their virginity by bathing the idol in some spring or river.[58] The tales of Helen's bathing in the two springs mentioned may have their origin in an old fertility rite.

The most convincing evidence in myth for identification of Helen as a fertility goddess is the fact that she is consistently being raped. Besides her "lawful" husband Menelaos, Helen had some relationship with numerous other men: Paris, Theseus, Enarsphoros the son of Hippokoon,[59] Idas and Lynkeus,[60] Korythos,[61] Deiphobos,[62] Achilles,[63] and even the son of Proteus, Theoklymenos.[64] Some of these stories may be late artistic elaborations, but the simple fact remains that in legand and literature what Helen is best known for is rape, and secondarily, perhaps, marriage. Her association with Theseus is particularly illuminating,[65] for the carrying-off of young ladies is one of his most characteristic activities. By the time he stole Helen,[66] he had already left Ariadne on an island, seen Phaidra hanged, and attempted to seize Persephone herself—in extant tradition, at least, a fruitless attempt. Nilsson [67] has demonstrated how

---

[56] VIII. 23. 4 ff.
[57] Kenchreai: Paus. II. 2. 3; Chios: Steph. Byz. s.v. Helene.
[58] E.g., Hera, Paus. II. 38.2.
[59] Plut. Thes. 31. 1 has Tyndareos entrusting her to Theseus to save her from Enarsphoros.
[60] Plut. Thes. 31. 1.
[61] In one of Parthenius' versions (34), he was the son of Alexandros and Oinone, not Helen; he fell in love with Helen at Troy and Alexandros killed him.
[62] Hinted at, δ 277, θ 517; Ilias Parva in Proclus, Chrest. ii ff.
[63] Paus. III. 19.11 ff has them dallying together on the island of Leuke; III. 24. 10 ff discusses the problem of whether or not Achilles was one of Helen's suitors; Kypria in Proclus Chrest. 1; Philostratus Her. XX. 32 ff tells of a temple of Helen and Achilles united by the Moirai.
[64] Euripides, Helen, passim.
[65] Kullmann, pp. 74-79.
[66] Plut. Thes. 31. 1: ἤδη δὲ πεντήκοντα ἔτη γεγονώς, ὥς φησιν Ἑλλάνικος, ἔπραξε τὰ περὶ τὴν Ἑλένην, οὐ καθ' ὥραν.
[67] Geschichte, p. 475 f.

the rape-motif is especially indicative of an origin as vegetation-goddess, and all of Theseus' ladies are certainly in that category. A quick consideration of Helen's history points to the conclusion that her style of life fits in perfectly with that of her Thesean counterparts. Some traditions [68] have the union of Theseus and Helen producing Iphigeneia, who also has some of the marks of a vegetation goddess.[69]

Erich Bethe long ago pointed out that, unlike a fertility goddess, who at one locality or another might have several husbands of different names, a respectable Greek lady could not have more than one consort simultaneously; therefore, certain genres like the epic introduce the rape motif in order to retain the tradition for all the known consorts of the goddess.[70] A further, perhaps civilizing, embellishment would be the story as Aristotle and his age had the option to tell it, that Helen was legally married to Menelaos, to Paris (δικαίως 'Αλέξανδρος ἔλαβε τὴν 'Ελένην, αἵρεσις γὰρ αὐτῇ ἐδόθη παρὰ τοῦ πατρός),[71] and to Deiphobos after Paris' death.

One other rather obscure myth is related in the works of Plutarch: [72]

λοιμοῦ κατασχόντος Λακεδαίμονα, ἔχρησεν ὁ θεὸς παύσασθαι, ἐὰν παρθένον εὐγενῆ κατὰ ἔτος θύωσιν. Ἑλένης δέ ποτε κληρωθείσης καὶ προαχθείσης κεκοσμένης, ἀετὸς καταπτὰς ἥρπασε τὸ ξίφος καὶ ἐς τὰ βουκόλια κομίσας ἐπὶ δάμαλιν κατέθηκεν· ὅθεν ἀπέσχοντο τῆς παρθενοκτονίας· ὡς 'Αριστόδημος ἐν τρίτῃ μυθικῇ συναγωγῇ.

The parallel with the Iphigenia story is striking, and so also is the more general implication that Helen could influence nature in some manner. Although a single such tale would not be grounds for establishing Helen as a vegetation-goddess, it is good support for the well-grounded rape-motif.[73]

Something about Helen's nature can be deduced, also, from an analysis of other divinities with whom she is associated or with whom she shares attributes or parallel myths. First, there is the

---

[68] E.g., Stesichorus and Euphorion in Paus. II. 22.6 f.
[69] Farnell, *Hero Cults*, pp. 55-58, cites the evidence.
[70] Erich Bethe, *Die Sage vom Troischen Kriege: Homer/Dichtung und Sage* III (Leipzig: Teubner, 1927), p. 106.
[71] Aristotle *Ars Rhetorica*, II. 1401 b 36.
[72] *Par. Min.* 35.
[73] C. Robert, *Die griechischen Heldensage*, Volume Two of L. Preller, *Griechische Mythologie* (Berlin: Weidmann, 1920), p. 339.

figure of Nemesis, Helen's mother in the *Kypria*.⁷⁴ Nemesis has a definite right to be called a goddess of vegetation, as Farnell has carefully pointed out: she takes the form of animals as Zeus pursues her over land and sea; the Nemesia, a funeral ceremony at Athens, may associate her with birth and death; a sculpture at Rhamnous has her holding a spray of apple in one hand, with a cup in the other and a stag in her crown; she is associated with Artemis through the titles of Oupis and Adrasteia.⁷⁵ Even her name, based on the root * nem-, should imply a pastoral connection.⁷⁶ The later residents of Ilion seem to have worshiped Helen under the title Adrasteia, a usual epithet of Nemesis.⁷⁷

Helen's association with Leda may be somewhat later (Homer is quite unclear about Helen's parentage aside from Zeus' being her father),⁷⁸ but both Nemesis and Leda lay an egg in one tradition or another,⁷⁹ and Pausanias identifies an egg tied up in ribbons at the sanctuary of Hilaeira at Sparta as the one Leda brought forth.⁸⁰ If this was the egg from which Helen was hatched, one wonders how it happened still to be whole; at any rate, the symbol of the egg is clearly associated with fertility, and may have come to be a representation of Helen's birth when some had forgotten what it originally signified. A third mother for Helen, attested in the Hesiodic corpus,⁸¹ is a daughter of Ocean. A connection with Ocean would be especially appropriate for a Sun-princess,⁸² and may have some bearing on the epic side of Helen, but apparently was not an element of the local Spartan context.

Helen's power is sometimes manifested in a manner suitable to a goddess of growth in beauty, like Aphrodite. Herodotus ⁸³ tells of a nurse bringing an ugly child to the temple of Helen at Therapnai. Helen herself appears and strokes the baby, the result being that

---

⁷⁴ VII Allen.
⁷⁵ Οὖπις for Artemis: Call. *Diana* 204; for Nemesis: IG 14. 1389 ii 2. Ὦπις for Artemis: Plato *Ax.* 371 a; Farnell, *Cults* II p. 488; Adrasteia: Chapouthier, *Les Dioscures*, p. 147; Farnell, *Cults* II p. 492.
⁷⁶ E. Laroche, *Histoire de la Racine NEM- en Grec Ancien* (Paris: Klincksieck, 1949), p. 89 f, notes the pastoral sense of νέμω and compares the Celtic goddess Nemetana.
⁷⁷ Farnell, *Hero Cults*, p. 324; Athenag. *Leg.* 1.
⁷⁸ Cf. pp. 47-49.
⁷⁹ See E. Bethe in Pauly-Wissowa s.v. Helene, 2826-7.
⁸⁰ III. 16. 1.
⁸¹ Fr. 24 M/W.
⁸² Cf. pp. 47 ff.
⁸³ VI. 61.

the child grows into the most beautiful in Sparta. A similar tale is is told by Pausanias,[84] that the wife of Ariston son of Agesikles had been the ugliest maiden in Sparta, but Helen changed her into the most beautiful. Ptolemaeus [85] also calls Helen the daughter of Aphrodite, and an Egyptian inscription from the time of Nero calls Helen the sister of Aphrodite.[86] The two have had a common experience, as well: Aphrodite, as she lies to Anchises in the *Hymn to Aphrodite* 117 f, says she was carried off from the χορός of Artemis; when Helen was raped by Theseus, she was sacrificing or dancing (χορεύω) at the sanctuary of Artemis Orthia.[87] Such a link is obviously remote, but what is interesting is the point in common: the dancing-floor of Artemis seems to be a good place to be raped from, and thus probably suggests more about Artemis than about the ladies who dance there.[88] Beyond the manifested powers of Helen and Aphrodite, of course, there is also the thematic connection that Aphrodite is always the bestower of beauty in myth, and Helen is always the woman most richly endowed with the same.

Another connection is with Eileithyia, to whom Helen is said to have dedicated a sanctuary in Corinth. Theseus and Peirithoos were off with the Thesprotians, and Helen had given birth to Iphigeneia, whom she later gave to Klytaimnestra and Agamemnon to care for.[89] Helen seems to have been in general a successful mother. Besides Hermione, the one child Homer allows her,[90] tradition mentions numerous others: Iphigeneia, daughter of Theseus; Korythos, Bounomos (or Bounikos), Idaios, and Aganos, the children of Paris;[91] and three children of unnamed father, Aithiolas,[92] Nikostratos, and Pleisthenes.[93] It seems certain that there must have been many more, as well.

Beyond all the relationships mentioned above, Helen has a close affinity to Artemis. Her very cult-center of the area around Sparta

---

[84] III. 7. 7.
[85] In Photius, *Bibliotheke* 149 A f Bekker.
[86] SEG 8. 500; Chapouthier, *REA* 42 (1940) 59-63, argues convincingly that the word ἀδελφή probably refers not to supposed blood-relationship, but to the common connection with beauty.
[87] Cf. Boedeker, 51-84, esp. p. 59.
[88] Cf. p. 58.
[89] Paus. II. 22. 7.
[90] § 12 ff.
[91] Dictys Cret. 5. 5; Tzetz. Lyk. 851; Nikander in Parthenius 34.
[92] Tzetz. Lyk. 851.
[93] *Kypria* IX Allen.

was also strongly dominated by the worship of Artemis Orthia. Theseus rapes Helen while she is dancing or sacrificing at the festival of Artemis Orthia in Sparta.[94] Carl Robert takes as significant the winged images and branches found in the temple at Therapnai, both types also having been found in connection with Artemis. To him the evidence implies a position of πότνια θηρῶν for Helen, too.[95] Artemis Iphigeneia, whom Hesychius identifies with Artemis,[96] was worshiped at Hermione, a place that may be intimately linked to the Helen legend.[97] Ptolemaeus says that Iphigeneia slew Helen and Menelaos among the Taurians (although perhaps it was really Thetis who did it in the form of a seal).[98] Artemis is called Ἄργη,[99] a title which immediately recalls Helen's epithet Ἀργείη in Homer.[100] Finally, if the Helenephoria is a festival connected with Helen, the carrying of baskets provides another link with the cults of Artemis, although baskets are certainly not restricted to her cults alone.[101] The strange cult of Artemis at Brauron, in any case, was marked by the carrying of baskets.[102]

In the discussion on κάνναθρα by Athenaeus,[103] the Spartan feast called Κοπίς "Cleaver" is mentioned. At this feast nurses take the male children to an image of Artemis Korythalia and there the boys have their private feast. Now, it appears that the original meaning of κόρος/κοῦρος should be not "adolescent," but "shoot" or "branch."[104] The extension of meaning is not surprising, considering how common is the comparison of a youth to a shoot or sapling; for example, Thetis says of Achilles:

... ὁ δ' ἀνέδραμεν ἔρνεϊ ἶσος (Σ 56).

---

[94] Plut. *Thes.* 31. 2; Hyg. *Fab.* 79.
[95] C. Robert, p. 337 f.
[96] S.v. Ἰφιγένεια.
[97] E. Bethe, Pauly-Wissowa, s.v. Helene, 2825.
[98] In Photius, *Bibliotheke* 149 A f Bekker.
[99] Farnell, *Cults*, 465, 487; Herod. IV. 34 f.
[100] Pp. 55-57.
[101] E.g., Demeter at Eleusis, Nilsson, *Geschichte*, p. 658.
[102] Cf. Mommsen, p. 458; cf. also Angelo Brelich, *Paides e Parthenoi* (Rome, 1970-5).
[103] IV. 138 e ff.
[104] Cf. Lysippus Comicus 9, *Et. Mag.* 276. 28. Also, s.v. κόρος in Hesychius; Frisk, pp. 920-1. The form of the reconstruction κόρος/κοῦρος: * korwos is actually attested in Linear B, spelled *ko-wo*; likewise the feminine * korwā, spelled *ko-wa* (see A. Morpurgo, *Mycenaeae Graecitatis Lexicon* pp. 165-6). The word * korwa is even attested in the classical period: κορϝ-α in IG V (2) 554.

Similarly, when Odysseus first talks with Nausikaa, he says he has never seen anything quite like her, except a young tree near the altar of Apollo on Delos (ζ 162 ff). Sappho follows the tradition in her description of the bridegroom:

τίῳ σ', ὦ φίλε γάμβρε, κάλως εἰκάσδω;
ὄρπακι βραδίνῳ σε μάλιστα εἰκάσδω (115 LP).[105]

Now, the root * korw- should survive as κορυ- before consonants; this form is attested in the words κορύ-διον "little κόρη,"[106] κόρυ-ξ "νεανίσκος,"[107] and κορυ-θάλη. The second part of the compound noun κορυ-θάλη is derived from θάλλω "sprout, thrive, grow,"[108] and the entire word is defined in the *Etymologicum Magnum*[109] as "laurel." Hesychius defines κορυθαλία as δάφνη ἐστεμμένη. τινὲς δὲ τὴν εἰρεσιώνην,[110] and Plutarch has εἰρεσιώνη defined as κλάδος ἀπὸ τῆς ἱερᾶς ἐλαίας ἐρίῳ λευκῷ κατεστεμμένος.[111] Further definitions[112] solidly connect the κορυ- of κόρος and κορυθάλη/κορυθαλία with branches of olive or laurel.

Another of Artemis' epithets is, of course, κουροτρόφος.[113] The scholiastic tradition of *Odyssey* τ 86 connects Κορυθαλία and Κουροτρόφος, in that an epithet of δάφνη is κουροθάλεια, διὰ τὸ κουροτρόφον τοῦ Ἀπόλλωνος. There is no need to invoke Apollo, since Artemis herself is known for the laurel.[114] Clearly the surface meaning of Κουροτρόφος is "nourisher of adolescents," and even κουροθάλεια may be interpreted as the "sprouter of adolescents" as well as the "sprouter of laurels." What is essential to note, however, is this fact: the Spartan feast of Tithenidia, where Artemis was invoked under the title Κορυθαλία, was an initiation rite for adolescents.[115] Implicit in the epithets Κορυθαλία and Κουροτρόφος is a metaphori-

---

[105] Cf. Hektor, Χ 87 and Telemachos, ξ 175.
[106] Naupaktos: *Journal of Hellenic Studies* 13 (1853) p. 346.
[107] Hesychius, s.v.
[108] Pindar has θάλος meaning "flowering garland" (*I.* 7. 24) and "offspring, child" (e.g., *O.* 2. 45, *O.* 6. 68, *N.* 1. 2); cf. ζ 155-7; and *H. Ceres.* 66. Boedeker, pp. 51-2 for a link between θάλος and the dance for a fertility goddess.
[109] 531. 53.
[110] S.v. κορυθαλία.
[111] *Thes.* 18.
[112] In the scholia to Ar. *Ploutos* 1054, εἰρεσιώνη is defined as a θάλλος ἐλαίας, ἢ δάφνης; cf. *Anecdota Graeca* 1. 246 Bekker s.v. εἰρεσιώνη.
[113] Cf. Diod. Sic. V. 73; Athenaeus 14. 645 A; G. Quinn, "The Sacrificial Calendar of the Marathonian Tetrapolis," Diss. Harvard, 1971, pp. 149-164.
[114] Witness her Lakonian epithet Δαφναία, e.g. Paus. III. 24. 8.
[115] Nilsson, *Geschichte*, p. 490.

cal comparison of the adolescent with the laurel sprout. Thus at Sparta Artemis is emphatically the local patroness of growth, human and vegetal.[116] Now, the κάνναθρα are used in the festival Hyakinthia,[117] and Artemis functions in some places under the name Ἰακυνθοτρόφος.[118] Hyakinthos, an old vegetation deity ousted by Apollo, has some importance around Sparta, represented by the festival and the fact that at Amyklai is situated his "tomb," at what became the sanctuary of Apollo.[119] These four Spartan figures, Helen, Hyakinthos, Apollo, and Artemis, are inextricably confused, if not originally identified or overtly connected. Sam Wide [120] and Carl Robert [121] compare the festival practice of the Κοπίς with the story of Helen making the child beautiful;[122] the implication might be that maidens were under the protection of Helen as boys were of Artemis.[123] A further connection with Artemis Korythalia could be Helen's son Korythos, who may have something to do with the district in Argos called ἐν Κορυθεῦσι.[124]

As is clear from the cases of Iphigeneia and Adrasteia, epithets and secondary names appear to be ever-shifting among Peloponnesian divinities. Could the outlandish pictures painted on Helen's κάνναθρα refer to a πότνια θηρῶν position, as Robert suggests? [125] In Hesychius, there is a Lakonian festival Therapnatidia, while θεράπνη is glossed as "θεραπαινίς, δούλη." [126] The relationship between Athena's name and that of her home-city, along with Helen's title Θεραπναίη νύμφη,[127] suggests that the title Θεραπναίη may stand in relation to the town as Ἀθηναίη does to Ἀθήνη; that is, there may exist the sequence Name-of-divinity → Name-of-city → Adjectival name-of-divinity, with the town named originally for Artemis in her

---

[116] H. Jeanmaire, *Couroi et Couretes* (Lille, 1939), 521 ff and *passim*; also C. M. Bowra, *Greek Lyric Poetry*² (Oxford, 1961) p. 35.
[117] Cf. p. 68.
[118] Nilsson, *Geschichte*, p. 317.
[119] *Geschichte*, pp. 316 f.
[120] Wide, p. 343.
[121] Robert, p. 337.
[122] Herodotus VI. 61.
[123] Wide, p. 344 cites Theocritus XVIII as further evidence with the Dromos of the song somehow connected with Helen's cult; cf. M. J. Mellink, *Hyakinthos* (Utrecht: Kemink en Zoon N.V., 1943), p. 55.
[124] Paus. VIII. 54. 5; Mellink, 114 ff shows that Helen among many was raped during a time when she was picking flowers.
[125] Robert, p. 339.
[126] S.v. Θεραπνατίδια, θεράπνη.
[127] Tryphiodorus 520.

role of κουροτρόφος. Again, no single fact may prove Artemis' close relationship with Helen, but an accumulation of such circumstances becomes convincing.

The longer and more closely one considers thematic and cult parallels between various goddesses of the Peloponnese, the more confused the identities of the ladies become. Farnell goes so far as to claim that Artemis, Hekate, Demeter, Persephone, and Aphrodite are all "cognate." [128] To his list one may be justified in adding the more minor figures Iphigeneia, Ariadne, Kallisto, Nemesis, and others. Furthermore, Helen has a great deal in common with some of them—notably Artemis, Nemesis, Iphigeneia, and Ariadne, but more than likely with Demeter also [129] and certainly with her often-raped "daughter" Persephone.

It is perhaps appropriate here to mention the Proto-Corinthian aryballos of the Louvre,[130] which shows a clearly hieratic female figure (she is larger than all the other figures, her head projecting beyond the border of the painting, arms held up in the usual hieratic psi-pose) being grasped on the wrist by a male to the right, with another male, sword in hand, to his right, and two figures on horseback to the lady's left. The painting has been interpreted logically enough as Helen, Theseus, and Peirithoos, with the Dioskouroi confronting their sister's ravisher (the painter may be telescoping events, for the tradition as we have it does not allow Theseus and the Dioskouroi to come into direct conflict). It may well be true that this painting represents the Helen-Theseus myth, but it is also apparent that the rape-motif is an artistic type, for it seems to be represented also on a Geometric krater in the British Museum,[131] which features a large boat with many crewmen inside and a disproportionately large man and woman boarding it, the woman holding a wreath in her hand. Some scholars have interpreted this picture as Helen and Paris, while others take it to represent Theseus and Ariadne. It is impossible to make a sure identification. The problem of these paintings illustrates again the fact that the further back these myths are pushed, the less distinct the differences between goddesses become. On the basis of all the similarities between

---

[128] *Cults*, II. 425.

[129] C. Picard, *Les Religions Préhelléniques* (Paris: Presses Universitaires de France, 1948), p. 188 notes the similarity between them in their cult practices, Thesmophoria and Helenephoria.

[130] Ca. 680 BC, Louvre CA 617.

[131] From Thebes; Br. Mus. 1899. 2-19.

Helen and her Peloponnesian neighbors, then, it seems safe to assert that Helen is one form, one local variant, of the ancient Mediterranean fertility goddess.

One word of caution seems appropriate here: just because several divine figures are cognate, it does not necessarily follow that they are identical. A goddess of vegetation and animal fertility was worshiped simultaneously at many places and thus was known by many names and developed many independent sets of myths and cults. Even a figure who is seemingly an offshoot of another, such as Kallisto, need not abandon her special mythology to Artemis, the goddess from whose original nature she evolved.[132] The separations into local variants of the fertility goddess happened early, and by the time of any written record at all she is already known through a rich array of local myths. Thus Helen's identity does perhaps derive from the Mediterranean nature goddess, but this origin does not change the fact that early in time she was no longer thought to be cognate with any of her neighbors around Lakedaimon.

Thus it is with a sense of arguing an unnecessary point that we return for the last time to the problem of Helen's name. The formation NOUN + φόρια, as in Helenephoria, is a common one for festivals throughout Greece, and some of the noun-portions of the festival names are cult-titles or whole names of divinities, as in Νικηφόρια, a Pergamene festival of Athena Nikephoros,[133] Σκιροφόρια, a festival of Athena at Athens,[134] and Δαφνηφορία, a festival of Apollo held at various places.[135] Besides Athena's cult title Nikephoros there exists also a title, practically a separate entity Nike. Σκιράς is the old name of Salamis [136] and also the title of Athena on Salamis, in Phaleron, and at Skiron.[137] The Daphnephoria is a festival of Apollo, but there exists in myth an entity Daphne, as well.

It has been shown that the word ἑλένη must mean "reed," "shoot," or the like. At the Helenephoria there are carried baskets called

---

[132] W. Sale, *Rheinisches Museum für Philologie* N.F. 108 (1965) 34.
[133] SIG 629, 24, ii BC.
[134] Aristophanes *Thes.* 834, *Ek.* 18, 59, etc.
[135] Apollo Daphne-phoros: Anacreontea 11. 6 Bergk; at Athens, CIA III. 278, 720 a; Phyle, Plut. *Them.* 15, Theophr. ap. Athen. X. 424 f; Eretria *Ephem. arch.* 1869, 404 a, 1892, 121, etc.; Chaironeia CIG 1595. See also Farnell, *Cults* IV 124 f; 284f; Paul Stengel in Pauly-Wissowa s.v. Daphnephoria.
[136] Strabo IX. 1. 9.
[137] Salamis, Herod. VIII. 94; Phaleron, Strabo IX. 1. 9, Paus. I. 1. 4, I. 36. 4; Skiron, Pollux IX 96.

ἐλέναι. The etymology of Helen's name, then, may be one or possibly a combination of the following:

(1) If the vegetation goddess in Lakedaimon—nameless, or named Artemis or perhaps Demeter or Kore—were celebrated with a festival where baskets called ἐλέναι were carried (as Artemis was celebrated at Brauron, and Demeter in Attica and elsewhere), it is conceivable that on the basis of such parallels as Skirophoria : Skiras and Daphnephoria : Daphne, the word Helenephoria could originally have meant "the carrying of baskets," and come to mean rather "the carrying of the divine entity 'Ελένη." The case of the Daphnephoria is instructive here, for the myth of Apollo and Daphne is late,[138] while Apollo's association with the laurel is definitely early.[139] It seems likely that the mythological figure of Daphne is a back-formation on Apollo's more general association with laurel. Helen could have resulted, then, from a back-formation on the Mediterranean fertility goddess' association with baskets.

(2) ἐλένη can be interpreted as meaning essentially "shoot, sprig," with this meaning derived from the common denominator of "wicker" and "reed." In the figure of Kore there is an adequate parallel of a vegetation goddess with a similar name: κόρος originally means "shoot," and even the meaning "youth" or "adolescent" is derived from the basic vegetal concept.[140] There is also Hyakinthos, an old Peloponnesian god *and* the name of a plant, as well.[141] Thus ἐλένη "shoot" could be a logical name for a vegetation goddess. The lady, then, as well as the plant, would be a product ultimately of the root * wel- "twist," a root intimately connected with the process of growth. Helen's name thus may be a cognate of the English word "willow." [142]

The etymology may be carried back as far as either suggestion (the latter, of course, being truly at the root of the matter) and still result in a viable meaning for the goddess' name. Whichever is correct, the Spartan Helen is a nature divinity, associated with growing things, and she is closely related to other manifestations of the fertility goddess of the Mediterranean, who is elsewhere celebrated by the carrying of baskets.

---

[138] Ovid, *Met.* I. 452 ff; Parthenius, XV.
[139] *H. Ap.* 396.
[140] Cf. pp. 75-77.
[141] Cf. Mellink, *passim*.
[142] *American Heritage Dictionary* s.v. * wel- in Calvert Watkins' index of Indo-European roots.

CONCLUSION

The Helen who has emerged from these studies is a complex character, and at first glance she may appear to be too complex and even too contradictory to be assigned a single nature. In Homeric epic she is drawn as a terrible, beautiful woman with remarkable powers which she uses both to benefit and to destroy the people who surround her. She is the cause of the Trojan War, and a symbol of the quest for undying fame, but this fame involves danger, even death. She is the lady who can help Odysseus spy on Troy and then turn around and use her wiles in an attempt to thwart the Greek plot to conquer by means of the Horse. She is closely associated with Aphrodite, a goddess whose threats are as terrible as her gifts are desirable. In all the action of Homer, Helen is the woman who is at once menacing and irresistibly beautiful.

The Homeric diction, a more subtle layer in the entire makeup of the epic picture, presents Helen as more overtly divine, with epithets and attributes that would seem to connect her with her Indo-European forebears. She is related to the Dioskouroi, who are clearly Indo-European in mythological origin, and thematically has much to do with Dawn—replaced by Aphrodite in epic—and the Sun-princess. Moreover, the descendants of this Indo-European Sun-princess display an ambivalent nature which parallels Helen's overt character in the artistic contexts of the *Iliad* and the *Odyssey*. The epic picture, then, appears to hang together as a neat package: although the author of an individual epic makes use of the Helen-figure for his own ends, nevertheless her character is largely defined by the traditional elements of the epic genre, which point toward Indo-European origins of themes and characters as well.

The shreds of evidence regarding Helen's cult, however, present her more as an earth goddess, localized primarily around Sparta, presiding over the fertility of the inhabitants of her domain. She is no artistic construct, but a powerful religious reality who is dealt with as a personal divinity.[1] In fact, she may be worshiped in a

---

[1] Aside from archaeological evidence of Helen's worship, note the traces of serious religious consideration of her in Euripides, *Helen* 1451-1511, Aristophanes, *Lysistrata* 1296-1315, Theocritus XVIII, and possibly in the fabled background to Stesichorus' *Palinode*. Some helpful treatments of post-

manner reminiscent of many of the old Mediterranean goddesses, particularly Demeter/Kore and Artemis. We have, then, on the one hand a traditional Indo-European epic figure with remote divine origins, but whose essential divinity has been eroded through countless years of artistic treatment; and on the other a pre-Indo-European fertility goddess whose power is still manifest at Sparta and elsewhere, and whose worship must be taken seriously. How can these two apparently different Helens be reconciled?

The answer begins with the fact that the Sun-princess of the Indo-European Dioskouroi is historically a deity of the third function, a fertility goddess.[2] Such an identification should not be difficult to accept, for it is clear that the Sun is a life-giving force. The mythology surrounding the Sun-princess involves continual rape and recovery, as she disappears and reappears again. The Twins are responsible for bringing her back each time, and the Dioskouroi-Helen-Theseus myth fits this pattern well. With the coming of epic, certain relationships in the Dioskouroi-Helen mythic motifs were no longer acceptable, and so as Helen was whisked further and further from her Lakonian home, her "brothers" the Dioskouroi were replaced by her husband and his brother, Menelaos and Agamemnon, and their followers, the Argives, men from the bright land where Helen lived.

This kind of rape-recovery motif has an obvious parallel in the activities of fertility goddesses such as Demeter/Kore. Every year the vegetation goddess must disappear and reappear, and thus the convention of the rape-recovery motif must be assigned to her, as well. A syncretism of the Sun-princess and the similar fertility deities is then easy to understand. Both types spend much of their time out of sight, under the earth, and reappear regularly. Although their religious origins may not be equivalent, the mythical reflexes of their natural rhythms are comprehensibly similar.

Finally, a goddess who spends half her time in the dark—either under the earth or in the night sky—necessarily becomes associated with sinister powers. If indeed Helen is an epic reflex of such a being, her magic and her dangerous unpredictability as far as the

---

Homeric literary representations of Helen include C. Wolff, "On Euripides' *Helen*," *HSCP* 77 (1973) 61-84; J. Hamilton, "The Function of the Helen Figure in Euripidean Drama," Diss. Minnesota 1973; C. Segal, "The Two Worlds of Euripides' Helen," *TAPA* 102 (1971) 553-614; and R. J. Groten, "The Tradition of Helen in Greek Literature," Diss. Princeton 1955.

[2] Wikander, "Légende," p. 52.

Argives go may stem from this aspect of her nature. In fact, any nature goddess will be terrible and unpredictable much of the time, and so Helen's Homeric character is directly compatible with her divine antecedents. Her relationship to both light and dark probably explains her later association with the moon, as well.[3]

Thus Homer's Helen is a composite of motifs from both Indo-European and Mediterranean religion and mythology. Clearly she must receive her name only after the Sun-princess has entered Greece and contacted local fertility deities who are closely related to growing things. From the blend of Indo-European and pre-Indo-European elements eventually emerges an identity whose natural disappearance and reappearance challenges the artistic imagination to create a setting in which she may exist most colorfully. Nagy has shown that the hexameter, the fabric of Homeric epic, is a Greek and not a common Indo-European invention, which must come into being just as these Greek and Mediterranean religious elements are making contact for the first time.[4] Helen is, then, a rare example of the synthesis of Indo-European and Mediterranean in the context of the hexameter. Because she was such a colorful figure, perhaps, and because she was not so universally powerful a goddess as an Artemis or Athena or Demeter/Kore, she was carried into the epic genre as its most exalted heroic lady, precariously bridging the gap between divine and human realms. If Wikander is correct, and the Indo-European epic heroes are frequently anthropomorphizations of archaic religious figures, then Homeric epic should be heavily populated with such former divinities. The case of Helen, which is more overt than most, should serve as an example of a process whereby this transition may be effected.

---

[3] There is some association between Helen and the Dawn in Theocritus XVIII 26-31, although it would be impossible to know for certain whether this association is a vestige of epic motif or a literary elaboration of artistic and cult tradition. Clearly, the entire Idyll identifies Helen with themes of marriage and fertility. Another literary reference to Helen and the Dawn may possibly be found in Alcman's *Partheneion*, on which see Bowra, *Greek Lyric Poetry*, pp. 51-55.

[4] Nagy, *Comparative Studies*, Chapter III.

INDEXES

I. GENERAL INDEX

Achilles 5, 6, 10-12, 15, 18-20, 22, 24, 31, 32, 46 n. 8, 56, 59 n. 54, 71, 75
Adrasteia 62, 73, 77
Agamemnon 9, 10, 20 n. 30, 22 n. 31, 26-29, 31, 35, 40, 43, 46 n. 8, 50-52, 74, 82
Aigisthos 27
Aillil 9 n. 12
Aithre 61
Ajax 5, 9, 27, 31 n. 11
Alcman 49 n. 16
Alexandros (cf. Paris)
Amory, A. 12 n. 20
Amyklai 68, 77
Anchises 12 n. 19, 74
Anderson, W. S. 33 n. 13
Andromache 9 n. 10, 11, 15, 16, 41
Antinoos 18, 31
anthropomorphization 1-3, 50, 83
Aphrodite 12-14, 16, 17, 19, 24, 25, 34, 36 n. 18, 41, 43, 46, 53, 54, 58, 61, 62, 73, 74, 78, 81
Apollo 26, 76, 77, 79, 80
Apollodorus 31 n. 11
Ares 36 n. 18, 62
Arete 41
Argeia 62
Argos 47, 55, 57, 62, 70, 77
Ariadne 58, 61, 70, 71, 78
Aristophanes 76 n. 112, 79 n. 134, 81 n. 1
Aristotle 72
Artemis 41, 43, 53, 54, 59-62, 71, 73, 74, 76-80, 82
    Artemis, Brauronian 66, 67, 75, 80
    Artemis Iphigeneia 75
    Artemis Korythalia 75, 77
    Artemis Orthia 69, 74, 75
Astyanax 30
Aśvins 49-51
Athena 20 n. 30, 25, 27, 28, 33 n. 13, 41-43, 47, 53-55, 58 n. 52, 62, 77, 83
    Athena Nikephoros 79

Athenaeus 53 n. 37, 63 n. 5, 65, 66, 68, 75, 76 n. 113
Athenagoras 69 n. 48
Atreidai 11, 50 n. 28, 51, 53
Atreus, House of 29, 46, 47

baskets 65-69, 75, 80
Bethe, E. 50 n. 23, 72, 73 n. 79, 75 n. 97
Beye, C. R. 34 n. 16
Boedeker, D. D. 54 n. 40, 74 n. 87, 76 n. 108
Boisacq, E. 19 n. 29, 64
Bowra, C. M. 77 n. 116
Brauronian Artemis (cf. Artemis, Brauronian)
Brelich, A. 75 n. 102
Briseis 11, 15, 42
Butterworth, E. A. S. 33 n. 13, 52 nn. 35 and 36

Calhoun, G. M. 25 n. 2
Callimachus 73 n. 75
Casaubon, J. 66
Catalogue of Ships 9
Chadwick, J. 46 n. 6
Chantraine, P. 46 n. 7, 56 n. 46, 59 n. 54, 61 n. 61, 64
Chapouthier 63 n. 4, 73 n. 75, 74 n. 86
Chryseis 42
Chryses 51
Conchobar 9 n. 12
Cross, T. P. 9 n. 12
Cú Roi 9 n. 12
Curtius, G. 63 n. 2

Daphne 79, 80
Daphnephoria 79, 80
Dawkins, R. M. 69 n. 42
dawn 49, 81
dawn-goddess 53-55
Deiphobos 34, 71, 72
Demeter 36 n. 18, 42, 75 n. 101, 78, 80, 82, 83
Demodokos 36 n. 18

INDEXES

Detienne, M. 7 n. 6, 8 n. 9
Dictys 74 n. 91
Dihle, A. 61 n. 62
Diodorus Siculus 76 n. 113
Diomedes 21, 54 n. 41
Dioskorides 66
Dioskouroi 10, 47, 48, 53, 55, 56, 78, 81, 82
  horsemen 51, 56
  immortality of 48, 49, 51, 52
  light and dark alternation 49, 51
  rescuers 50, 52, 61
  and Sun 50, 62
Diphilus 66, 67 n. 27
divá(s) duhitár 53
divinity 24-26
dogs 17, 18, 46, 47
Dolon 10 n. 12
Draupadi 51
Due, O. S. 60 n. 57
Dumézil, G. 1-3
Durante, M. 7

egg 73
Eileithyia 74
Elysium 39
Eos 53, 54
Erekhtheus 54 n. 41
Eumaios 29, 36 n. 18
Euphorion 72 n. 68
Euripides 1, 61 n. 63, 71 n. 64, 81 n. 1
Eurykleia 37, 43
Eustathius 52, 69 n. 48
evening star 49

faded god 1-3
Farnell, L. R. 1, 2, 55 n. 43, 63 n. 1, 72 n. 69, 73, 75 n. 99, 78, 79 n. 135
Faust, M. 17
Fergus 10 n. 13
fertility goddess 1, 70-82
Frame, D. 18 n. 26, 27 n. 5, 49 n. 18, 56 n. 47
Frisk, H. 19 n. 29, 46 n. 7, 56 n. 46, 59 n. 54, 64, 75 n. 104
Furtwängler, A. 48 n. 14
generic epithet 44, 45
Ghali-Kahil, L. B. 63 n. 4
Grégoire, H. 64
Groten, R. J. 82 n. 1
Güntert, H. 49 n. 17

Hades 20 n. 30, 62
Hamilton, J. 82 n. 1
Hekabe 11, 58 n. 52
Hekate 78
Hektor 8, 11, 15, 16, 19-22, 30, 31, 76 n. 105
Helen
  and Achilles 6
  and Aphrodite 12-17, 25, 40, 46, 47, 54, 73, 74, 81
  and Ariadne 71, 78
  and Artemis 29, 59-61, 69, 74-78
  beauty of 12, 16, 23, 25, 73, 74, 81
  cult of 68-70, 81, 82
  and death 19, 20, 22, 23
  and Demeter 78
  divinity of 2, 3, 12, 39, 40, 55, 62, 63, 70, 81
  dual nature of 12, 16, 17, 22, 23, 40
  in Egypt 39
  epithet system of 41-57, 62
  as fertility goddess 70-73, 77-82
  and Hera 46, 47, 59
  and Iphigeneia 72, 74, 78
  lament for Hektor 11, 21, 22
  name of 63-68
  and Nemesis 73, 78
  and Odysseus 33-35, 40, 53
  and Persephone 78
  and poetry 6-12, 32, 33, 81
  in Sparta 10, 24-40
  and sun 50, 53-55, 61, 62
  and Trojan Horse 34, 38, 40, 53, 81
  as wealth 28
  and weaving 7, 8
  witchlike powers of 32-34, 37-40
Helenephoria 68, 75, 78 n. 129, 79, 80
Helios 50
Hephaistos 46 n. 8
Hera 14, 15, 20 n. 30, 22 n. 31, 41-47, 55, 59, 62, 71 n. 58
Herakles 48
Hermes (Argeiphontes) 22 n. 31, 56, 57, 60
Hermione (city) 62, 75
Hermione (daughter of Helen) 24, 25, 74
Herodotus 39 n. 19, 69 n. 43, 73, 75 n. 99, 77 n. 122, 79 n. 137

Hesiod   52 nn. 32 and 33, 62 n. 64, 73
Hesychius   63 n. 5, 65, 69, 75-77
hexameter   83
Hippokoon   71
Hyakinthia   68, 77
Hyakinthos   77, 80
Hyginus   62 n. 64, 75 n. 94

Iasion   36 n. 18
immortality   26, 39, 40
Indo-European mythology   49
Indo-Iranian epic   1, 2
Iphigeneia   52 n. 36, 72, 74, 77, 78
Iris   6
Isocrates   69 n. 43

Jeanmaire, H.   77 n. 116
John the Lydian   63 n. 6

Kaibel, G.   70
Kakridis, J. Th.   7 n. 4, 28 n. 6, 34 n. 15, 35 n. 17
Kallisto   78, 79
Kalypso   8, 22 n. 31, 24, 36 n. 18, 39, 40, 42, 44, 46
Kanephoria   67
Kassandra   11
Kastor (cf Dioskouroi)
Kerberos   17
Kirke   8, 36 n. 18, 39, 44
Klymene   61, 62
Klytaimnestra   27-29, 35, 40, 43, 46, n. 8, 48, 52 n. 36, 74
Kock, T.   66, 67 n. 27
Kore (cf. Persephone)
Korythos   71, 74, 77
ko-wa   75 n. 104
ko-wo   75 n. 104
Kretschmer, P.   46 n. 6
Kullman, W.   61 n. 62, 71 n. 65

Laistrygonians   20 n. 30
Laroche, E.   73 n. 76
Latte, K.   62 n. 64
Leda   73
Leto   42
Leukippidai   50 n. 23
Linear B   59, 75 n. 104
Livy   69 n. 43
Lord, A. B.   2
Lysippus   75 n. 104

Macdonell, A.   49 n. 17, 50 n. 24, 51 n. 31
Mahābhārata   1, 2, 50
Mannhardt, W.   49 n. 19, 70
Maresch, G.   48 n. 14
Medb   9 n. 12
Megapenthes   30, 33
Meillet, A.   25 n. 3
Meleager   46
Mellink, M. J.   77 nn. 123 and 124, 80 n. 141
Menelaion   69
Menelaos   6, 7, 9, 10, 13, 14, 21 n. 30, 22 n. 31, 24-35, 37, 39, 40, 50-53, 55, 57, 72, 75, 82
Mommsen, A.   67, 75 n. 102
moon   63, 83
morning star   49
Morpurgo, A.   75 n. 104
Muellner, L.   33 n. 13
muse   33 n. 13, 41, 43

Nagler, M.   2
Nagy, G.   6 n. 3, 30, 31 n. 10, 49 n. 19, 53, 83
Nakula (cf. Pāṇḍavas)
Nāsatyā   49
Nausikaa   24, 25, 39, 41, 61, 76
Neanthes   63 nn. 3 and 5, 65
Nemesis   62, 73, 78
Nestor   27, 30
night   49
Nikander   74 n. 91
Nike   79
Nikostratos   74
Nilsson, M.   1, 58 n. 53, 65 n. 16, 70 n. 55, 71, 75 n. 101, 76 n. 115, 77 n. 118

Odysseus   9, 10, 15, 19, 20 n. 30, 21, 22 n. 31, 24, 25, 27-40, 53, 54 n. 41, 56, 76
O'Rahilly, C.   9 n. 12
Orestes   27, 28, 31 n. 11
Oupis   73
Ovid   80 n. 138

Page, D.   55 n. 44
Palmer, L. R.   59 n. 56
Pāṇḍavas   1, 2, 50-52
Paris   6-8, 12-16, 19, 21 n. 30, 22 n. 31, 23, 31, 39, 46, 50, 58 n. 52, 71, 72, 74, 78

Parry, M.   2, 9 n. 11, 44 nn. 1 and 2, 45 n. 4, 54 n. 42
Parthenius   71 n. 61, 74 n. 91, 80 n. 138
Patroklos   5, 22, 59 n. 54
Pausanias   52 n. 36, 61 n. 60, 62 n. 65, 69 nn. 43 and 47 and 48, 70, 71 nn. 57 and 58 and 63, 73, 74, 76 n. 114, 77 n. 124, 79 n. 137
Peisistratos   24, 30, 37, 53
Peleus   18
Penelope   7, 15, 21 n. 30, 23 n. 31, 28, 31, 35-40, 43-45, 53, 61
   dream of 37, 38
Persephone   43, 53, 71, 78, 80, 82, 83
Phaethon   62
Phaiakians   25, 26, 58, 59
Phaidra   70, 71
phantom   17
Phemios   31
Philostratus   71 n. 63
Photius   74 n. 85, 75 n. 98
Picard, C.   78 n. 129
Pindar   49 n. 16, 50 n. 23, 76 n. 108
Pittheus   61
Plato   73 n. 75
Pleisthenes   74
Pliny the Elder   65 n. 18
Plutarch   8 n. 9, 61 n. 59, 65 n. 16, 68, 69 n. 48, 71 nn. 59 and 60 and 66, 72, 75 n. 94, 76
Pokorny, J.   64, 68
Pollux   65-68, 79 n. 137
Polybius   69 n. 43
Polydeukes (cf. Dioskouroi)
Poseidon   20 n. 30, 33 n. 13, 36 n. 18, 43, 45, 48, 61, 62
potnia   59
Preller, L.   72 n. 73
Priam   9, 10, 19, 56, 57
Proclus   71 n. 62, 63
Prometheus   62
Proteus   27, 39, 71
Ptolemaeus   74, 75

Quinn, G.   76 n. 113

Rhadamanthys   39, 51 n. 31
Robert, C.   72 n. 73, 75, 77
Robertson, C. M.   1
Rose, H. J.   1, 61 n. 63, 62 nn. 67 and 68

Sahadeva (cf. Pāṇḍavas)
St. Elmo's Fire   63
Sale, W.   79 n. 132
Sappho   76
Schachermeyr, F.   51 n.31
Schlerath, B.   18 n. 26
Schmidt, J.   48 n. 14
Schmitt, R.   7 n. 8, 58 n. 38
Scott, J. A.   7 n. 6
Segal, C. P.   9 n. 10, 11 n. 17, 18 n. 26, 82 n. 1
Selene   41
Simonides   8
Sinon   10 n. 13
Skiras   80
Skirophoria   80
Slover, C. H.   9 n. 12
Sophocles   31 n. 11
Stanford, W. B.   8 n. 8
Stengel, P.   66, 79 n. 135
Stephanus of Byzantium   69 n. 48, 71 n. 57
Stesichorus   52, 72 n. 68, 81 n. 1
Strabo   79 nn. 136 and 137
Styx   19
suitors
   of Helen   10, 52
   of Penelope   28, 35
sun   49, 50, 61, 62, 82
sun-princess   49, 50, 53, 55, 62, 73, 81-83
Sūryā   49, 50
Sūryã   49, 50

Teichoskopia   6-12
Telemachia   24
Telemachos   21 n. 30, 24-30, 32, 35, 37, 53, 54 n. 41, 57, 76 n. 105
Theocritus   48 n. 13, 69 n. 47, 70, 77 n. 123, 81 n.1
Theoklymenos   71
Theophrastus   65
Therapnai   69, 70, 73, 75
Therapnatidia   77
Theseus   48, 50, 61, 71, 72, 74, 75, 78, 82
Thesmophoria   78 n. 129
Thetis   31, 41, 42, 75
Thompson, M. S.   69 n. 44
Tithenidia   76
Tryphiodorus   69 n. 43, 77 n. 127
Tyndareos   47, 48, 71 n. 59
Tzetzes   74 nn. 91 and 92

Uşas 53, 54
Vedic mythology 49-51
Vendryes, J. 25 n. 3
Ventris, M. 46 n. 6
Venus 64
Vergil 50 n. 28
Vernant, J. P. 7 n. 6

Watkins, C. 80 n. 142
weaving 7-9
Webster, T. B. L. 18 n. 28
Whallon, W. 2, 55 n. 45

Whitman, C. H. 5 n. 2, 7 n. 5, 11 n. 16, 15, 29 n.7, 56 n. 49
Wide, S. 50 n. 22, 69 n. 48, 70 n. 55, 77
Wikander, S. 1-3, 50 nn. 26 and 27, 52 nn. 34 and 35, 82 n. 2, 83
Wolff, C. 82 n. 1

Xenophon 68

Zeus 14, 20 n. 30, 22 n. 31, 26, 45-48, 54, 55, 57, 59, 62, 73

II. GREEK WORDS

ἄεθλος 7
'Ἀθηναίη 77
αἰνῶς 12
ἀμβρόσιος 59
ἀμφίπολοι 41
ἄναξ 51
ἀοιδιάω 8
ἀοίδιμος 8
ἀοιδός 7, 32
ἀπαγχομένη 71
'Ἀργείη 42, 55-57, 62, 75
ἀργεννή 58
Ἄργη 75
ἀργής 58
ἄργος 58
Ἄργος 46, 57
ἀργός 47, 56
ἀστεροπή 57 n. 51
ἄχολον 32-33
ἄχος 32
ἄχος ἄλαστον 31-32

βοῶπις 44, 47

γλαυκῶπις 47

Δαφναία 76 n. 114
δάφνη 76
Δαφνηφορία 79
δενδρῖτις 70
δῖα γυναικῶν 43, 45
δῖος 57
Διὸς ἐκγεγαυῖα 42, 54
Διὸς θυγάτηρ 43, 53-55
Διὸς κούρη 41, 47, 52, 54, 55
δμωαί 41

ἐᾱνός 58, 59, 61
ἐᾱνός 59, n. 54

εἰανός 59, n. 54
εἶδος 61
εἴλη 64
εἰρεσιώνη 76
ἑλάνη 63, 65-67
'Ἐλένεια 65, 68
ἑλένειον 65
ἑλένη 63-68, 79, 80
'Ἐλένη 63-65, 68, 70-72, 80
'Ἐλενηφόρια 65-67
ἑλένιον 64-66
ἑλένιος 65
ἕλη 67 n. 31
ἕλος 64, 65
ἐπιλήθεται 32, 33
ἐπίληθον 32, 33
ἔρις 18
ἕρκος 9
εὐεργός 28
εὐπατέρεια 43, 45

ἠέλιος 57
ἠλακάτη 60, 61
ἠλέκτωρ 57
'Ἠλύσιον 39, 51 n. 31
ἠυκόμος 42, 45, 46

θάλλω 76
θάλος 76 n. 108
θεραπαινίς 77
Θεραπναίη νύμφη 69, n. 43, 77
θεράπνη 77

'Ἰακυνθοτρόφος 77
ἱστόν 60
'Ἰωκή 19

κακομήχανος 17-18
καλλίκομος 43, 45
καλλιπάρηος 42, 45

Καλλιστεῖα 65
Καλλίστη 65
κάνναθρα 68, 75, 77
κλέος 6, 10-12, 17, 30-32
  κλέα ἀνδρῶν 6, 32
  κλέος ἄφθιτον 31
Κοπίς 75, 77
Κόρεια 65
κόρη 76
Κόρη 65
κούρη Διός (cf. Διὸς κούρη)
κοῦρος 75-76, 80
κορύδιον 76
κορυθάλη 76
κορυθαλία 76
κόρυξ 76
κουροθάλεια 76
κουροτρόφος 76, 78
κρυερός 19
κρυόεις 18
κυνώπης 43, 46
κυνῶπις 30, 43, 46, 47
κύων 17, 47

λευκώλενος 41, 43-45

νέεσθαι 56
νεκτάρεος 58, 59
νηπενθές 32, 33, 40, 53
Νικηφόρια 79
νόστος 6, 12, 31, 35, 56
νύμφα 44, 46

ξανθός 51

ὀθόνη 58, 59, 61
ὀκρυόεις 18

παλλακίς 43
παμφανόωντα 25, 57
πελώριος 9
πένθος 30-33
  πένθος ἄλαστον 31, 32
πορφύρεος 7
πόσις 42, 45
πότνια 44
  πότνια θηρῶν 75, 77

ῥιγεδανῆς 19-22, 42, 47
ῥῖγος 22

σέβας 25
σέλας 64
σελήνη 63-65
Σκιράς 79
Σκιροφόρια 79
στεροπή 57
στεροπηγερέτα 57
στρωφάω 60
στυγερή 19-22, 44, 47
στυγέω 19
στύξ 19

τανύπεπλος 41, 45

ὕβρις 18
ὑπερίων 57

φαεινός 58
φιλότης καὶ εὐνή 36
Φοβός 18
φρίσσω 21
φυή 61

χαλκός 57
χορός 74
χρυσηλάκατος 29, 60

III. PRINCIPAL PASSAGES CITED

Hesiod

  Theogony 27-28: 33 n. 13
      98-103: 32
  Fr. 197. 4-5 M/W: 10
  Fr. 204. 87-89 M/W: 10
  Fr. 357 M/W: 7 n.8

Homer
  Iliad
  A 16: 51
    59-60: 56
    375: 51
  B 286-288: 56

Γ 97-100: 31
  125-128: 6-7
  156-160: 12
  178-179: 9
  243-244: 48
  324-325: 22
  351-354: 22 n. 31
  385: 58
  399-412: 13, 19
  414-417: 13
  419-420: 58
  433-436: 14
  438-446: 14
Δ 8: 55

197: 31
207: 31
E 908: 55
Z 318-320: 15
326: 15
344-358: 16, 17
491: 60
Θ 366-370: 20 n. 30
I 64: 18
257-258: 18
401-409: 12
412-416: 5-6
Ξ 314-328: 14
Σ 56: 75
Υ 61-66: 20 n.30
Ω 437-438: 57
773-775: 21

Odyssey

α 357: 60
δ 14: 24
45-46: 25
71-75: 25
90-103: 26
108-110: 31
120: 33 n. 13
128-129: 29
131: 60
135: 60
145-146: 30
221-226: 32

238-239: 33
259-264: 34
274-276: 34
561-569: 39
ε 61-62: 8
θ 457: 25
κ 221-222: 8
226-227: 8
λ 298-304: 48
427-434: 27
436-439: 27
502-503: 20 n. 30
ν 399-400: 20 n. 30
ξ 68-71: 29
117: 29
π 418: 18
τ 570-581: 38
583-587: 38
φ 351: 60
ψ 213-224: 23 n. 31, 35-6
ω 192-202: 28

Hymns

Venus 16-17: 60
117-118: 60
xxvii. 1: 60

Linear B

Py Fr 1225: 59

Sappho

Fr. 115 LP: 76

www.ingramcontent.com/pod-product-compliance
Ingram Content Group UK Ltd.
Pitfield, Milton Keynes, MK11 3LW, UK
UKHW042005230426
12048UKWH00009B/567